CW00833106

100 DESI STORIES

WISDOM FROM ANCIENT INDIA

100 DESI STORIES

WISDOM FROM ANCIENT INDIA

Madhur Zakir Hallegua

JAICO PUBLISHING HOUSE

Ahmedabad Bangalore Chennai
Delhi Hyderabad Kolkata Mumbai

Published by Jaico Publishing House
A-2 Jash Chambers, 7-A Sir Phirozshah Mehta Road
Fort, Mumbai - 400 001
jaicopub@jaicobooks.com
www.jaicobooks.com

© Jaico Publishing House

100 DESI STORIES: WISDOM FROM ANCIENT INDIA
ISBN 978-81-8495-855-3

First Jaico Impression: 2016
Second Jaico Impression: 2017

No part of this book may be reproduced or utilized in
any form or by any means, electronic or
mechanical including photocopying, recording or by any
information storage and retrieval system,
without permission in writing from the publishers.

Page design and layout: Jojy Philip, Delhi

Printed by
Trinity Academy For Corporate Training Limited, Mumbai

Contents

~ STORIES *on* Hinduism ~

1. The Favourite Disciple   3
2. The Fruit of True Devotion   5
3. Devotion Towards Parents   7
4. Emotion Is More Important Than Rituals   10
5. Pure Devotion   13
6. Help!   15
7. The Boatman and Shri Ram   18
8. The Superior Devotee   20
9. Saint Namdev and Vithoba   23
10. Brotherly Love   25
11. Karna, the Unparalleled Donor   27
12. Do What You Can   29
13. Rishi Bhringi and Prakruti   31
14. Bhasmasura and Mohini   34
15. Yudhisthir and the God of Dharma   36

16. In the Name of God   39

17. Parvati and the Crocodile   41

18. The First to be Worshipped — *Prathampujya* Ganesh   44

19. Ravana and Lord Shiva   47

20. Ramanand and the Mantra   49

21. The Mystery of the Broken Trunk   51

22. Can God Do It?   54

23. The Two Blessings of Krishna   56

24. Lord Narayan and Tulsi   58

25. Yudhisthir and the Dog   62

26. God's Plan   64

27. The King and His Belief in God   67

~ STORIES *on* Islam ~

28. The Wonderful Ways of Allah   73

293 Be With Me Allah!   75

30. The Sick Man   77

31. The Grapes   79

32. For Allah Only   80

33. Prophet Idris   82

34. Prophet Ibrahim and His Dream   84

35. Prophet Ayub   86

36. Prophet Dawood and His Lesson on Justice   89

37. God Gives Us Our Food   91

38. Syedna Hazrat Ibrahim   93

~ STORIES *on* Christianity ~

39. Where Are You, God?   99

40. The Value of Life   102

41. Know What You Need   104

42. Trust in God   106

43. Jesus and Zacchaeus   108

44. Daniel and the Lions   110

45. Elijah and the Priests of Baal   112

46. David and Goliath   114

47. Abraham and Issac   116

48. Jesus and the Woman Who Had Sinned   118

49. Balaam and His Donkey (Old Testament)   120

50. Job and God   122

51. The Spider and King David   124

52. Tom and the Gold Coin   126

53. King Solomon's Justice   128

~ STORIES *on* Sikhism ~

54. Guru Nanak and His First Deal   133

55. Lalo and Malik Bhago   135

56. Dunichand and the Needle   137

57. How Guru Nanak Chose His Successor   139

58. Guru Nanak's Last Message   141

59. Guru Nanak and the Fields   142

60. Guru Arjan   144

61. Mardana and Guru Nanak   146

62. God Himself Helps Us   148

63. The Panj Pyare   150

64. Guru Tegh Bahadur and the Imposters   152

65. Humayun and Guru Angad Dev Ji   154

66. Nanak and His Thread Ceremony   156

67. Guru Nanak and the Bowl of Milk   158

68. The Successor of Guru Amar Das   160

69. Guru Nanak and the Non-Vegetarian Food   162

70. Nanak and the Fields of Grain   164

71. Lehna and the Fruits   167

72. Guru Nanak and the Guard   170

73. Guru Nanak and the Sesame Seed   172

꙳ STORIES *on* Buddhism ꙳

74. Increase Your Periphery   177

75. Let My Son Live!   179

76. Gautam Buddha and the Brahmin   181

77. Buddha and the Young Men and Women   183

78. Prince Sattva and the Tigress   185

79. Prince Siddharth and the Swan   187

80. Women in the Sangha   189

81. Buddha's Visit to Kapilvastu   191

82. Buddha and the Elephant   193

83. Buddha and Amrapali   195

84. The Right Path to Happiness   197

85. Enlightenment for Everyone   199

86. Buddha and the Ignorant Students   201

87. A Farmer by Intellect   203

88. Buddha Achieves Nirvana   205

89. Buddha and King Bimbisara   207

 STORIES *on* Jainism

90. Lord Parshvanath   211

91. Lord Arishtanemi (Neminath)   214

92. Bharat and Bahubali   217

93. Anand and Gautamswami   220

94. The Statue of Bahubali   222

95. The Birth of Lord Sumatinath   224

∾ STORIES *of* SAINTS ∾

96. Shri Shankar Maharaj and the Doctor's God   229

97. When 'I' Die   232

98. All Creatures Belong to God   235

99. Sri Ramkrishna Paramhansa and the Scorpion   237

100. Sri Ramkrishna and the Idol of Krishna   239

STORIES

on

HINDUISM

1

The Favourite Disciple

Sukrut was the favourite disciple of his guru. Once, the other disciples confronted their guru and asked him why Sukrut was his favourite. The guru answered that instead of telling them, he would demonstrate the qualities of Sukrut which made him his favourite.

The next day, the guru gave one mango each to all his students. He told them to go to a place where nobody would be able to see them and eat their mango there. All the disciples left and came back after an hour or so.

Only Sukrut did not return. All the disciples along with the guru, waited for Sukrut. Finally, Sukrut came back late in the evening.

The disciples were surprised to see that not only had the favourite student come back late, he had also not eaten the mango. Now, the guru would surely be angry with him!

The guru asked Sukrut why he was late and why he hadn't eaten the mango. Sukrut replied and the other disciples understood why Sukrut was the guru's favourite student.

Pearls of Wisdom

1. What did Sukrut say?

2. What is the moral of this story?

To gain pearls of wisdom, try to answer these questions on your own before referring to the answers given below.

Answers

1. Sukrut said, "Guru*ji*, you had asked us to go to a place where there was nobody and eat the mango there. I went far and wide. But everywhere I went, I found that God was always with me. There was nowhere that I couldn't find His presence. So I couldn't eat the mango."

2. Whether we are aware of His presence or not, God is always with us. Those who live with this awareness indeed live enlightened lives.

2

The Fruit of True Devotion

King Uttanapad had two wives, Suniti and Suruchi. Though Suniti was calm and mature, the King loved Suruchi more than her. Suniti had a son called Dhruv and Suruchi's son was called Uttam.

One day, while they were both still young, Dhruv and Uttam went to sit on their father's lap. But Suruchi stopped Dhruv and said that in order to sit on his father's lap, he would have to be reborn as her son. Very cruelly, she asked him to get down from his father's lap. The King also did not stop her.

Dhruv was extremely hurt and went to Suniti. She consoled her son and asked him to pray to Lord Vishnu who would definitely help him.

In spite of being so young, Dhruv made up his mind and went into the dense forest and began to meditate on Lord Vishnu. He did not care about the wild animals, the darkness of the forest, nor his hunger and thirst. Single-mindedly, he concentrated on Lord Vishnu's name. After many years spent in deep meditation, Lord Vishnu was pleased with him. He appeared before him and told young Dhruv to ask him for what he wanted.

Dhruv said, "O Lord, please give me a place from which no one will ever ask me to get down."

——————— **Pearls of Wisdom** ———————

1. What did Lord Vishnu say?

2. What can we learn from this story?

To gain pearls of wisdom, try to answer these questions on your own before referring to the answers given below.

Answers

1. Pleased with his devotion, Lord Vishnu blessed Dhruv and said, "I am pleased with your devotion. I will grant you a place which no one has been given before and from where no one can ask you to step down. You shall be placed on the Pole Star from where you can look down on the whole world. Today onwards the Pole Star will be called '*Dhruv Tara.*'"

2. With supreme faith and devotion, a person can attain the highest position and honour that can be bestowed upon a human being. Once he had made up his mind, Dhruv no longer doubted his faith nor worried about his safety, hunger and thirst. Though he had initially longed only to be able to sit on his father's lap, through his steadfast devotion, he was granted a place which no man had ever been given before.

3

Devotion Towards Parents

A boy named Pundalik lived in a forest called Dandirvan. Though in his younger years he was devoted to his parents, the situation changed after he got married. He and his wife began to trouble his old parents.

Once, his parents decided to go to Kashi on a pilgrimage. He and his wife decided to accompany them. But here too, they ill-treated the parents. Young Pundalik and his wife rode on horses while his aged parents walked. The feeble parents were also given odd jobs to do.

They stopped to rest at Rishi Kukkutswami's ashram. At dawn, Pundalik heard a noise and saw young women wearing the dirtiest of clothes come into the ashram. They did all the odd jobs like cleaning the floor, washing the clothes, etc. But as they went out of the ashram after doing these chores, their clothes became beautiful and shone. Pundalik was surprised and even as he watched, they disappeared before his eyes.

Again at dawn the next day, the women came and completed all the chores. As they were about to leave, Pundalik asked them who they were. The women said, "We are the holy rivers Ganga, Yamuna and the others. Pilgrims come to us and wash away all their sins with our holy water. That is why our clothes are dirty."

One of them said, "But you Pundalik, are among one of the greatest sinners we have known!"

"What have I done?" asked Pundalik.

"Is it not true that you and that wife of yours ill-treat your aged parents? Is this why they brought you up with such love and affection?"

Hearing this, Pundalik realized his mistake. Then and there he decided to change. During the rest of the pilgrimage, his parents saw a drastic change in his and his wife's behaviour towards them. Pundalik had now truly become a devoted son to his parents.

Lord Vishnu who was watching this was extremely pleased with Pundalik's devotion. In His current avatar, He was Lord Krishna. He decided to visit Pundalik's house with His wife Rukmini and bless Pundalik.

But when Lord Krishna and Rukmini reached Pundalik's house, Pundalik was busy serving his parents. Even when he came to know that Lord Krishna had come to meet him, Pundalik refused to meet him before he had finished attending to his parents. Meanwhile, he threw a brick outside his house and told Lord Krishna to stand on the brick and wait for him.

After he had done his duty towards his parents, Pundalik came out to pay his respects to Lord Krishna. With great humility he begged His pardon.

Pearls of Wisdom

1. Did the Lord punish Pundalik for his insolence? What did the Lord say to him?

2. What can we learn from this story?

To gain pearls of wisdom, try to answer these questions on your own before referring to the answers given below.

Answers

1. In spite of being kept waiting by Pundalik, Lord Krishna was very pleased to see Pundalik's devotion to his parents. He stood on the brick that Pundalik had thrown and patiently waited for Pundalik. He gave Pundalik his blessings and told him that from now on, He would stay there and be called by the name of 'Vithoba' – the one who stood on the brick. Today, the temple of Lord Vithoba stands at this place and lakhs of people called *Warkaris* throng for a glimpse of Lord Vithoba on the day of Ashadhi Ekadashi.

2. Serving and respecting our parents is like serving and respecting God. God is ready to wait for a devotee who selflessly serves and does his duty towards his parents.

4

Emotion is More Important than Rituals

Lord Shiva is known to be the most kind-hearted of gods. It is very easy to win Him over with pure devotion.

A young boy from a lower caste was a devotee of Lord Shiva. He lived his simple life, doing the jobs that he was told. While doing them, his mind would be fixed on Lord Shiva. Since he was from a lower caste, he had no chance to be educated. He would chant Lord Shiva's name saying "Shava, Shava! Shava, Shava!"

Once, a Brahmin who was passing by heard him. On hearing, "Shava, Shava! Shava, Shava!" he was shocked to the core. He caught hold of the boy saying, "You fool! Do you know what you are chanting?"

"I am only taking the Lord's name," said the boy scared.

"Imbecile!" shouted the Brahmin. "You are chanting, 'Shava, Shava! Shava, Shava!' instead of 'Shiva, Shiva! Shiva, Shiva!' Do you not know, 'Shava' means dead body and 'Shiva' is the name of the Lord?!"

The poor boy was horrified to know this.

"Lord Shiva will punish you for this," cried the Brahmin.

The poor boy was now truly scared and begged the Brahmin's pardon saying, "Tell me what I should do now, O kind sir!"

"Now you must chant Lord Shiva's name correctly a hundred thousand times as penance. Say 'Shiva, Shiva! Shiva, Shiva!'" said the Brahmin and left.

Pleased at having done his duty, the Brahmin came home and worshipped Lord Shiva at his home. That night when he slept, he had a dream. He was sitting before the Shivalinga in his home and talking to Lord Shiva.

He said, "I am amazed at the ignorance of some people! How that illiterate boy was saying 'Shava, Shava' instead of taking Your sacred name! But I am glad that I have done my duty and brought his mistake to his notice. Now he will chant Your name correctly. I am glad that I have been a good devotee of Yours."

Lord Shiva replied, "That boy is a much superior devotee of mine than you are."

The Brahmin was horrified to hear this and said, "Why is that so, Lord?"

Pearls of Wisdom

1. What did Lord Shiva say?

2. What can we learn from this story?

To gain pearls of wisdom, try to answer these questions on your own before referring to the answers given below.

Answers

1. Lord Shiva said, "No matter what words the boy was using, there was only one emotion behind his words – to call out to me! He had no other intention. But your intention behind correcting him was to prove your superiority and to bring the boy's ignorance to his notice. The end result is that out of the fear of pronouncing my name wrongly and incurring my wrath, the poor boy has completely stopped taking my name. You have taken his devotion and turned it into fear! What kind of devotion is this?"

2. For God, emotion is more important than language, words, rites and rituals. He was pleased with the boy's devotion because the emotion behind it was absolutely pure. Whereas, though the Brahmin's words were correct, the emotion behind them was that of superiority.

5

Pure Devotion

Parvati, the daughter of King Himavan was undergoing severe austerities as she wanted to marry Lord Shiva. She had given up her palace and had gone to live in the forest. She had also given up her royal robes and ate only leaves for survival. She created a Shivalinga out of mud and worshipped it with all her heart. Daily, she would say her prayers and offer flowers to the Shivalinga.

One day, a group of hunters stopped by the Shivalinga. When they saw her, their leader asked her if they could offer prayers and offerings to the Shivalinga. Parvati replied that indeed they could and that it would be her privilege to have them worship the Shivalinga.

Pleased, the hunters began to do the *puja*. Their leader brought out some meat that he had brought with him and began to offer it to Lord Shiva. Shocked, Parvati stopped him.

"How can you defile the holy Shivlainga with meat?" she demanded. "Do you not know that milk and *bel* leaves are to be used as offerings for the Shivalinga? Not doing so is against the prescribed rituals of worship."

The hunter answered, "Lady, we are hunters. We only have meat with us which we have hunted and cooked ourselves. We can only offer that to the Shivalinga and then partake it."

"No!" said Parvati. "I cannot allow you to offer meat to the Shivalinga."

"Why don't you let us try to offer the meat, Lady?" asked the hunter. "If Mahadev does not accept it, we shall leave." Saying so, the hunter offered the meat to the Shivalinga.

———————   **Pearls of Wisdom**   ———————

1. What happened next? Did Lord Shiva accept the offering?

2. What is the moral of this story?

To gain pearls of wisdom, try to answer these questions on your own before referring to the answers given below.

Answers

1 & 2. To Parvati's surprise, Lord Shiva accepted the offering of the meat. In reality, Lord Shiva had Himself appeared as a hunter before Parvati to teach her an important lesson. If Parvati wanted to marry Shiva, she needed to understand that for Lord Shiva, a person's devotion was more important than the rites and rituals performed. If the devotion is pure, even an offering like meat becomes pure and is accepted by Lord Shiva.

6

Help!

In the fateful game of dice, Yudhisthir wagered and lost everything – his kingdom, his riches, his brothers, himself and Queen Draupadi to Duryodhana.

Once Draupadi was won, Duryodhan ordered his brother Dushyasana to bring Draupadi to the court. He also mentioned that if she didn't come on her own, he should drag her and bring her. When Dushyana brought her to the court, Duryodhan announced that now Draupadi was his servant as Yudhisthir had lost her in the game of dice and so now he was her lord and master. It was a matter of great shame for a woman to be brought that way to the court.

Not content with this, the evil Duryodhana ordered his brother Dushyasana to disrobe her. A helpless Draupadi looked towards her five warrior husbands expecting them to protect her. But as Yudhisthir had lost them and himself too in the game of dice, they too had become servants of Duryodhana. They stood helpless, hanging their heads in shame. A distraught Draupadi then appealed to the elders of the family – King Dhritarashtra, Bhishma, Guru Drona and Kripacharya to stop Dushyasana and protect her. But they too cited that as she had been lost by Yudhisthir, they could not stop Duryodhana and help her.

Draupadi then appealed to everybody else present in the court to protect her, but no one dared stand up against Duryodhana. Seeing that now Draupadi was completely helpless, Dushyasana pulled at her sari.

Draupadi then called out to Lord Krishna for help. "O Yogeshwar! Please help me. Save my dignity!" On hearing her prayer, Lord Krishna immediately came to her help and miraculously added layers and layers of cloth to her sari. Dushyasana kept pulling her sari for as long as he could but the cloth of her sari simply did not end. At last, he could pull no longer and fell to the ground exhausted.

After that incident had passed, Draupadi asked Lord Krishna, "Why didn't you come to my aid as soon as you knew I needed help?"

———————— **Pearls of Wisdom** ————————

1. What did Lord Krishna answer?

2. What is the moral of the story?

To gain pearls of wisdom, try to answer these questions on your own before referring to the answers given below.

Answer

1. Lord Krishna said, "Draupadi, you called your five husbands, the elders in the family and everyone else in court for help. How could I interfere at that time? But the moment you called me, I came to your aid."

2. This happens to most of us. We trust that our family, our loved ones and people we know will come to our help. But they might not even be in a position to help us when we need their help. We call everyone we know except for God. God is everywhere and the moment we call out to Him, He rushes to our aid. We must make it a habit to make God our partner and call out to Him for help.

7

The Boatman and Shri Ram

This story is of the time when Shri Ram, Sita and Lakshman were on their way to the forest to go into exile. While on their way, they came across the river Ganga. A boatman was ferrying people and the three of them sat in his boat.

The boatman was extremely happy to meet them. Once they reached the other side, Shri Ram asked the boatman, "What should I give you for bringing us across the river?"

"My Lord," said the boatman, "just like two doctors or two barbers do not charge each other for their services, since both of us are boatmen, I cannot charge you for this boat ride."

Shri Ram was surprised to hear the boatman's answer. "My dear man," he said, "that you are a boatman is true, but how is it that I am a boatman?"

─────────── **Pearls of Wisdom** ───────────

1. What was the boatman's answer?

To gain pearls of wisdom, try to answer the question on your own before referring to the answers given below.

Answer

1. The boatman said, "My Lord, I am a boatman who ferries people across the river. But you are the boatman who ferries people from darkness to light and from ignorance to enlightenment. Hence, not only are you a boatman, you are the most superior boatman in the world."

8

The Superior Devotee

Devrishi Narad was proud of his devotion to Lord Vishnu. Since he always chanted Lord Vishnu's name, he felt that there couldn't be a superior devotee than him in the entire universe. Lord Vishnu knew that he had to do something about the matter.

Once when Devrishi Narad came to meet Lord Vishnu, the Lord casually asked him if he had met one of His ardent devotees on Earth. Narad wondered who could be such an ardent devotee of the Lord. "Who is this man, O Lord?" he asked. Lord Vishnu told him and Narad left to meet this man.

To his intense surprise, he found that the devotee whom the Lord had spoken of was nobody special. He was an ordinary farmer. However, Narad decided to observe him for a whole day to find out more about him. He found that after the farmer awoke, he would chant the name of the Lord. After completing his work and before going to bed, he would once again thank the Lord for His guidance, support and love.

When Narad met Lord Vishnu the next time, he asked Him, "Lord, your devotee prays to you only twice in a day while I constantly chant your name. So how can he be your ardent devotee and not I?"

Lord Vishnu smiled. He said, "If you are a true devotee, please do as I say. I will give you a bowl of oil. Please give it to Lord Shiva in Kailash. However, please make sure you don't spill even a drop of the oil."

Lord Vishnu gave him a bowl filled up to the brim with oil. Narad had to use his entire concentration to ensure that he did not spill the oil. After he came back, Lord Vishnu asked him if he had been successful in his task. Narad proudly told Him how he had had to concentrate to ensure that not even a drop of oil was spilt and how he had been successful at his task.

Lord Vishnu then asked him a question which completely destroyed his pride.

Pearls of Wisdom

1. What did Lord Vishnu ask Narada? What happened then?

2. What is the moral of this story?

To gain pearls of wisdom, try to answer these questions on your own before referring to the answers given below.

Answers

1. Lord Vishnu asked him, "While going about your task, did you chant my name like you usually do? And what about the time when you had gone to Earth? How many times did you chant my name then?"

Narad remembered that he had completely forgotten to chant the Lord's name while undertaking both the tasks. Lord Vishnu then said, "Narad, I asked you to carry a little bowl and you forgot me in your anxiety. The poor farmer carries plenty of tensions of his own day to day life but still remembers me twice a day. So now tell me who is the superior devotee?"

2. Only God is capable of understanding each person's devotion completely. Since we cannot understand the true extent of another person's devotion, we should refrain from commenting on it and labelling ourselves as superior to others.

9

Saint Namdev and Vithoba

Saint Namdev was a great devotee of Lord Shiva. His greatest desire was to be with Lord Shiva permanently. One day, he had a dream in which Lord Shiva appeared and directed him to go to a nearby temple. "Go and meet my devotee, Vithoba, in the temple. See what you can learn from him," He said.

When Saint Namdev reached the temple, he asked the priest where he would find Vithoba. The priest pointed out to an old man. On seeing him, Saint Namdev couldn't believe his eyes! Vithoba was sitting with his feet on the statue of Lord Shiva.

Walking towards Vithoba, a shocked Saint Namdev wondered how a person who disrespected Lord Shiva could be His devotee.

Vithoba saw Saint Namdev coming towards him and said, "O Saint! I am sitting with my feet on Lord Shiva's statue. But I am very old and it hurts me to even move. Please help me and move my feet to a place where Lord Shiva isn't there."

Saint Namdev was even more surprised but he held Vithoba's legs and tried to move them. To his immense surprise, he found that no matter where he placed the old man's legs, Lord Shiva appeared there!

On seeing this, Saint Namdev realized his mistake and begged Vithoba for forgiveness. He had learned his lesson at last!

──────────── **Pearls of Wisdom** ────────────

1. What was the lesson Saint Namdev learnt from Vithoba?

2. Why did Saint Namdev beg forgiveness?

To gain pearls of wisdom, try to answer these questions on your own before referring to the answers given below.

Answers

1. Saint Namdev desired to be with Lord Shiva at all times. But from Vithoba he learned that contrary to what he thought, Lord Shiva is present everywhere in the entire universe. He understood how he could be with Lord Shiva and experience His presence everywhere and at all times.

2. Saint Namdev had made the mistake of underestimating Vithoba's devotion because he did not conform to Saint Namdev's standards of devotion. That is why he begged for his forgiveness.

10

Brotherly Love

Laxman was known for his unconditional love and devotion to his brother Shri Ram. This was the time when Ram, Sita and Lakshman were back from their exile.

Kalapurusha had come to meet Shri Ram. Shri Ram asked Lakshman to stand guard outside his room and to allow absolutely no one to enter. He also told him that anyone who came in and interrupted the meeting would be given the death sentence.

Unfortunately, Rishi Durvasa chose that very moment to enter the palace. He had come to meet Shri Ram. Lakshman tried to tell him that Shri Ram had given strict orders to not allow anyone to enter the room.

On hearing this, Rishi Durvasa was enraged. He warned Lakshman that if he did not inform Shri Ram of his arrival, he would curse Shri Ram and his brothers.

Lakshman thought for a while. Then, in spite of knowing that he would be given the death sentence, he went in to the room to see Shri Ram and interrupted his meeting.

Pearls of Wisdom

1. What did Lakshman think?

2. What is the moral of the story?

To gain pearls of wisdom, try to answer these questions on your own before referring to the answers given below.

Answers

1. Lakshman knew that true to his word, Rishi Durvasa would curse Shri Ram and his brothers if he was not allowed to meet Shri Ram. He thought that instead of all his brothers dying from Rishi Durvasa's curse, it was better for him to die and thus, his brothers would be spared.

2. One can easily understand the unconditional love and devotion Lakshman had towards his brothers and especially towards Shri Ram. Even when he faced imminent death, he did not hesitate to do his duty towards his brothers.

11

Karna, the Unparalleled Donor

Karna, the great *Mahabharata* warrior, was also known as *Daanveer* Karna – the great donor. Once, Arjuna asked Krishna, "What is it about Karna that makes him such a great and ideal donor? Why am I not known to be equal to him in this respect?"

Lord Krishna smiled and decided to teach Arjuna why. They were passing by some mountains. With a snap of his fingers Lord Krishna turned the mountains to gold. Then he said, "Arjuna, you must give away these mountains of gold to the people of this village. Only, ensure that every bit of the gold is given away."

Happily, Arjuna called the villagers, announcing that he would be donating gold. This made them very happy and they followed him to the mountains of gold, singing his praises. Arjuna proudly took his place and began to give away gold to each of the villagers. This went on for two days. However, the gold simply did not reduce. Arjuna was tired. He told Lord Krishna that he wanted to rest as it was now impossible for him to donate any more gold.

Then Lord Krishna called Karna and told him to donate the mountains of gold and ensure that all the gold was distributed.

—————— **Pearls of Wisdom** ——————

1. How did Karna distribute the mountains of gold?

2. What is the moral of this story?

To gain pearls of wisdom, try to answer these questions on your own before referring to the answers given below.

Answers

1. Karna simply called out to the villagers, told them to take the mountains of gold and left.

2. Even though Arjuna gave away the gold, he was actually fascinated by it. So he involved himself in giving it away to the villagers. He gave each villager the amount that he thought was right. He was also happy with the villagers' praise of him. Karna, however, just gave away the mountains of gold without expecting any praise or blessings from the people. Thus, he proved himself an unparalleled donor.

12

Do What You Can

Shri Ram, Lakshman, Hanuman and their army of monkeys wanted to cross the mighty sea to reach Lanka and free Devi Sita from the clutches of Ravana. The Lord of the Seas asked Shri Ram to build a bridge across the vast sea so that they could cross over and reach Lanka.

The *Vanar Sena* (the army of the monkeys) set to work finding stones to build a bridge which would carry all of them. But when they put the heavy stones they had collected into the water, they began to sink into the sea. Hanuman then inscribed the name of Shri Ram on each stone, and then the stones floated on the water.

Seeing the *Vanar Sena* building a bridge, a little squirrel began to work too. It began to carry little pebbles. But the monkeys became irritated with it. "Move out of the way or I'll trip over you," said one. "Don't bother, your efforts aren't going to help anyway," said another.

The committed squirrel, however, said, "I am doing my bit to help build the bridge. Let me do what I can to serve Shri Ram. I am not as big as you all but I can carry small pebbles. My work will be of use to you."

Shri Ram was moved by the squirrel's words and he stroked the little creature's back. (It is said that this is why squirrels have three lines on their back.) He told the monkeys, "Devotion matters more than size or strength. Not only is the squirrel's work useful, it is extremely necessary as well."

──────── **Pearls of Wisdom** ────────

1. Why was the squirrel's work important?

2. What can we learn from this story?

To gain pearls of wisdom, try to answer these questions on your own before referring to the answers given below.

Answers

1. The monkeys had forgotten that in order to keep the bridge together and ensure that it did not collapse, they needed little pebbles to be placed in between the stones. Thus, the squirrel's work was not just useful, but extremely necessary as well.

2. No task is unimportant or mean. Each person, animal, plant or living being makes its own contribution in the larger scheme of things. Each piece of work is a service to God. We must respect each individual's work and allow them to contribute and serve God.

13

Rishi Bhringi and Prakruti

Once, the rishis organized a Gyan Sabha where they asked Lord Shiva and Goddess Parvati to teach them about 'Purusha' and 'Prakriti'.

"'Purusha' and 'Prakriti' combine and create the universe. 'Purusha' represents the male element, and 'Prakruti', the female element in any being. I represent the male element – 'Purusha' and Parvati represents the female element – 'Prakruti'," said Lord Shiva. "Neither is more important than the other. Both combine and complement each other in the formation of every being in the universe," He continued.

However, there was one rishi called Bhringi who disputed this fact. He said, "Lord, You are all-encompassing, You are whole, You are the entire universe Yourself. If that is so, why is it not enough to only worship You? Even before Your marriage to Goddess Parvati, we worshipped You alone. Why then is the worship of Goddess Parvati along with Your worship necessary now?"

Lord Shiva explained to him that since the beginning of creation, Purusha and Prakriti had actually been one. But in order to create the universe, Lord Brahma had needed the help of Prakriti and had asked Lord Shiva to separate Himself from Prakriti so that He could create the universe with Her help. So Purusha and Prakriti had always been together and neither was inferior or superior to the other.

But Rishi Bhringi was not convinced. At the end of the *Gyan Sabha*, all rishis asked Lord Shiva and Parvati for their permission to circumambulate them together as Purusha and Prakriti. Everyone did so except for Rishi Bhringi. He only circumambulated Lord Shiva, signifying that neither was he was willing to accept Goddess Parvati as Prakriti nor did he feel Prakriti was of any importance in the world. Both Lord Shiva and Parvati said nothing.

Rishi Bringi then told Lord Shiva that he was not satisfied with circumambulating Him only once. He wanted to go around Lord Shiva once more. The Lord agreed. This time, Lord Shiva and Parvati turned into their *Ardhanareeshwar* form (half-male, half-female) so that Rishi Bhringi would understand that both Purusha and Prakriti were to be circumambulated together.

However, Rishi Bhringi took the form of a bee and only went over Lord Shiv's head and not Goddess Parvati's. Goddess Parvati then asked him, "So, you do not accept that Prakriti is as important as Purusha?" "No," he replied. "Well so be it!" she replied. "I curse you that all the elements of Prakriti shall disappear from your body!"

———————— **Pearls of Wisdom** ————————

1. What happened when the Prakriti element left Rishi Bhringi's body?

2. What is the moral of the story?

To gain pearls of wisdom, try to answer these questions on your own before referring to the answers given below.

Answers

1. As Lord Shiva had said, our body too consists of elements of both Prakriti and Purusha. When the elements of Prakriti left Rishi Bhringi's body, his body became a heap of sand. It was left with no form since all the watery elements dried up from his body.

2. As Lord Shiva said, we must accept that both the male and female elements make up our body and none is inferior to the other.

14

Bhasmasura and Mohini

Once there was an asura named Bhasmasura. He was not very intelligent, but he wanted to become powerful. He performed great austerities to please Lord Shiva. After many years, Lord Shiva was pleased and appeared before him. "What do you desire, Bhasmasura?" asked Lord Shiva.

Bhasmasura replied, "I wish that whosoever I put my right hand on, shall immediately be reduced to ashes."

"*Tathastu*," said the Lord.

Then Bhasmasura saw Goddess Parvati. She was so beautiful that Bhasmasura wanted to marry her. Since she was already married to Lord Shiva, he decided that he would burn up Lord Shiva and marry the Goddess. So he tried to put his hand on Lord Shiva's head but Lord Shiva moved away from him. But Bhasmasura was determined to marry Goddess Parvati and kept following Lord Shiva everywhere.

Lord Shiva called out to Lord Vishnu for help. Lord Vishnu took the form of Mohini, the enchantress. Mohini was so beautiful that Bhasmasura immediately fell in love with her and asked her to marry him. Mohini told him that she would do so but on one condition. She was an accomplished dancer and wanted to marry an accomplished dancer.

She told him that they would have a dance contest. If Bhasmasura could copy her dance moves, she would gladly marry him. Bhasmasura readily agreed.

Mohini began to dance. Bhasmasura began to copy her moves.

———————— **Pearls of Wisdom** ————————

1. Why did Mohini ask Bhasmasura to dance?

To gain pearls of wisdom, try to answer the question on your own before referring to the answer given below.

Answer

1. Bhasmasura was trying to copy Mohini's moves and so he let his guard down. In the course of the dance, Mohini put her right hand on her head. Without thinking, Bhasmasura also put his right hand on his head and went up in flames.

15

Yudhisthir and the God of Dharma

Yudhisthir was known for his righteousness. Even during his rule, he was known to be righteous and just. He always followed the path of Dharma.

After losing the game of dice a second time with Duryodhana, Yudhisthir had to go into exile with his four brothers (Bheem, Arjun, Nakul and Sahadev) and Queen Draupadi. Once during their exile, the Pandava brothers and Draupadi felt very thirsty. Yudhisthir, the eldest Pandava, asked his youngest brother Sahadev to go and look for water. Sahadev went and found a lake. But as he tried to drink water, a *yaksha* appeared before him and said, "This is my lake, you must answer my questions first. If you give me the correct answers, you can drink the water, otherwise you can't. If you drink the water without my permission, you will fall down dead!"

But Sahadev was too thirsty and dismissed the *yaksha's* words. He scooped up the water in his palms, drank from it and fell down dead. When Sahadev didn't return for a long time, Yudhisthir sent his another brother Nakul to look for Sahadev and also to fetch water. When Nakul did not return, Yudhisthir sent Arjuna and then Bheem to find the others.

When Bheem too did not return, he went to look for his brothers. He came across the lake and found all his brothers dead beside the lake.

"Who killed my brothers?" asked Yudhistir. "I did," said the *yaksha*. "This is my lake. You can drink this water only after answering my questions. If you don't answer my questions and drink the water, you too shall die like your brothers."

"I will try to answer your questions to the best of my ability," said Yudhisthir humbly. Then, the *yaksha* asked Yudhisthir many questions which Yudhsithir correctly answered.

The *yaksha* who was actually the God of Dharma and Yudhisthir's father, was pleased and told Yudhisthir that he could ask for any one brother of his to be restored to life.

Yudhisthir then asked for Nakul to be restored to life.

The *yaksha* was surprised and said, "Yudhisthir, do you not know that Bheem and Arjun are mightier than Nakul? Either one of them can be of help to you to win the impending war. Why then did you ask for Nakul to be restored to life?"

-------------------- **Pearls of Wisdom** --------------------

1. Why did Yudhisthir ask for Nakul to be restored to life?

2. What is the moral of this story?

To gain pearls of wisdom, try to answer the question on your own before referring to the answer given below.

Answer

1. Yudhisthir told the *yaksha*, "I have two mothers. My own mother Kunti and Mother Madri. Nakul and Sahadev are

Mother Madri's sons. For me, there is no difference between both my mothers. So it is only fair that if I, the son of Mother Kunti am alive, one of Mother Madri's son's should also be alive."

2. Yudhisthir was indeed a righteous person. He knew that he would be much more powerful against the Kauravas with Bheem or Arjun beside him. But still he chose Dharma over everything else and asked for Mother Madri's son to be restored to life.

16

In the Name of God

This was the time when Lord Ram had come back to Ayodhya after the exile. Devrishi Narad and a few other rishis were pondering over the supremacy of taking God's name as compared to God Himself. Rishi Narad decided that he would ask Hanuman for his help as he was a devotee of Lord Ram.

Rishi Narad told Hanuman that he wanted to conduct a test. He asked Hanuman to do something which would anger the guru of Lord Ram. Then the Lord's guru would definitely ask Lord Ram to punish Hanuman.

Hanuman acted in a way that angered Lord Ram's guru. The guru called Lord Ram and instructed him to punish Hanuman the next day by shooting arrows at him. This greatly saddened Lord Ram as even he couldn't understand Hanuman's behaviour. With a heavy heart, he accepted the guru's punishment for his devotee.

The next day, everyone in the kingdom gathered to see Hanuman being punished by Lord Ram. Lord Ram aimed at Hanuman and shot an arrow. The arrow went towards Hanuman but fell to the ground instead of hitting him.

Pearls of Wisdom

---

1. Why did the arrow not hit Hanuman?

2. What is the moral of the story?

To gain pearls of wisdom, try to answer the questions on your own before referring to the answers given below.

Answers

1. Hanuman was standing with his eyes closed, his mind fixed on Lord Ram. He was chanting Lord Ram's name. Since the Lord's name was more powerful than the Lord Himself, the Lord's name protected Hanuman and he came to no harm.

2. *Namasmaran*, or chanting God's name, is more powerful than God Himself and is the best way to protect oneself from all troubles in life.

17

Parvati and the Crocodile

This is a story around the time when Parvati had undertaken severe austerities to attain Lord Shiva as her husband. She knew that in her last birth, she was His wife, Sati. But to attain Him again in this birth, she would have to increase her spiritual powers to become capable of becoming His wife. As days passed by, she progressed closer towards her aim.

When she reached the last stage of her austerities, Lord Shiva decided to test her. He asked two rishis to appear before her in the form of a crocodile and a boy. The rishis agreed and while Parvati was walking, suddenly she saw a huge crocodile holding the leg of a little boy in its fierce jaws.

"Save me! Somebody save me!" cried the little boy. Parvati saw the little boy and was filled with concern for him. She addressed the crocodile saying, "O crocodile, please leave this boy. He is so young. He has not even lived half his life and you are about to kill him? Please let him go. What harm has he done to you?"

To this the crocodile replied, "How can I let him go? He is my food. You talk of saving his life, but if I don't eat, I too will die. If you find me some food, I shall let him go."

"From where can I find you food, O crocodile?" asked Parvati.

"Why? You can be my food yourself! I can live on you for days together. You decide. It's either you or the boy."

───────────── **Pearls of Wisdom** ─────────────

1. What did Parvati say?

2. What happened next?

3. What is the moral of this story?

───

To gain pearls of wisdom, try to answer these questions on your own before referring to the answers given below.

Answers

1. Parvati said, "I have been doing austerities to attain Lord Shiva. But if I were to die instead of this child, after my death, my soul will anyway merge into the Supreme Soul of Lord Shiva. So my sacrifice will not go in vain. Also, if I want to become Lord Shiva's wife, it is my duty to ensure the survival of life on Earth, even if it is at the cost of my life. Eat me, O crocodile, and spare the poor boy."

2. Saying this, Parvati sat with her eyes closed, with Lord Shiva's name on her lips, ready to die for the little boy. Any moment, she expected the crocodile to devour her. But instead, both the crocodile and the boy appeared as rishis and told her that they had come to test her. They blessed her and said that she had passed the test with flying colours.

3. Parvati wanted to be Lord Shiva's wife. She understood that

as His wife, it was her duty to share His responsibilities of ensuring the survival of the species on Earth without thinking about her own life. She also understood that merging into Lord Shiva is the final truth of every soul and even if her life ended, she would definitely reach her goal of attaining Lord Shiva.

18

The First to be Worshipped – *Prathampujya* Ganesh

Goddess Parvati had told Ganesh that in order to control his hunger, he must meditate and worship his father daily before eating his food. Ganesh did so regularly.

Once, all the gods decided that they had to appoint a god who would be Prathampujya – the one who would be worshipped the first before everybody else. But who among them should be chosen for the position? Should it be Indra – the king of Gods or Surya, the brightest among them; or Vayu Dev, the Wind God; or Varun Dev, the God of Water; or should it be Kartikeya, the Commander of the divine forces; or Ganesh, the God of Intelligence and the most auspicious of them all?

To decide the matter, all the gods went to Lord Shiva. It was decided that all the gods would undertake a trip around the entire universe. The god who came back first from the trip would be declared the 'first one to be worshipped' – *Prathampujya*.

All the gods lined up to begin the race – Indra on his elephant, Kartikeya on his peacock, Ganesh on his mouse, and other gods on their various mounts. When the race began, all the gods raced ahead on their respective mounts. However, since Ganesh's mount was a mouse, he couldn't catch up with the others. Soon Ganesh and his mount were lagging behind. His mount gave up trying to race ahead.

Suddenly, Ganesh also realized that since Vayu Dev, Surya Dev, Chandra Dev and all the other gods were out on the trip, the balance of the universe had been disturbed as none of the gods had thought about who would carry out their work during their absence.

Ganesh decided to do something about it. He went about maintaining the balance in the universe. Just as he had put it into place, both Lord Shiva and Parvati came up to him and asked him what he was doing there. Ganesh replied that he was maintaining the balance of the universe in the absence of the gods.

He then asked Lord Shiva and Parvati to be seated at their place. Then he began his worship of Lord Shiva. After finishing his worship, he told his parents that he would circumambulate them. So while Lord Shiva and Parvati sat, Ganesh went around them with his hands folded. Lord Shiva smiled.

Just then, one by one, all the gods began to return. Karthikeya arrived first, followed closely by Indra. A hot debate began among them as to who had reached first. When all the rest had arrived, they requested Lord Shiva to announce the winner.

To everyone's surprise, Lord Shiva declared Ganesh the winner of the competition. The gods reacted furiously. "Why him? I didn't even see him anywhere around me," said Indra. "I reached first, Father," said Karthikeya.

Then Lord Shiva said, "Ganesh is the first even though he did not actually venture out for the race. Secondly, he also deserves to be the *Prathampujya* for two more reasons."

───────────── **Pearls of Wisdom** ─────────────

1. Why did Lord Shiva say that Ganesh was first? What were the two other reasons?

2. What is the moral of this story?

───

To gain pearls of wisdom, try to answer the questions on your own before referring to the answers given below.

Answers

1. Lord Shiva had smiled when Ganesh had gone around Him and Parvati. He knew that Ganesh was doing so because for him, his parents were the whole universe. Thus, Ganesh was the first to finish his trip around the universe. Secondly, Ganesh also did two important things:

   a. In the absence of the gods, he went beyond the call of duty and maintained the balance of the universe, and

   b. Obeying what his mother had told him, he had completed his worship of his father too.

2. Unlike the other gods, Ganesh was not power-hungry. He was creative and intelligent. Through his actions, he achieved three things at the same time. With creativity, intelligence and prudence, all problems in the world can be solved.

19

Ravana and Lord Shiva

Ravana had cut off his ten heads and offered them to Lord Shiva. Pleased with his devotion, Lord Shiva blessed him saying, "Ravana, you are my most superior devotee."

This pleased Ravana no end and the praise went to his head. He started behaving arrogantly and began to look down upon the other devotees of Lord Shiva. Once when he had gone to Kailash to meet Lord Shiva, he insulted Nandi by calling him a monkey. A furious Nandi cursed him that soon he would be defeated by a mere monkey.

Ravana on his part told Nandi that he was so strong that, if he wished, he could lift Mount Kailash and take it to Lanka. Nandi warned him that such arrogance would surely bring about his downfall. But Ravana paid no heed to Nandi and began to lift Mount Kailash.

Lord Shiva was watching all this. Ravana had just lifted Mount Kailash a little when Lord Shiva pressed his toe on the ground. Ravana's fingers were jammed under the weight of Mount Kailash and he could lift it no longer.

—————————— **Pearls of Wisdom** ——————————

1. If Lord Shiva had called Ravana his most superior devotee, why did He not allow or help him to lift Mount Kailash and prove his strength?

To gain pearls of wisdom, try to answer the question on your own before referring to the answer given below.

Answer

1. Lord Shiva had praised Ravana when Ravana had deserved praise. He did not want Ravana to look down upon and insult others or brag about his abilities because of it. Just because one has been blessed by God, it does not mean that one should become proud and arrogant.

20

Ramanand and the Mantra

A young man called Ramanand enrolled in an ashram to study under a guru. The guru gave him a mantra. The next day, Ramanand gathered around 400-500 villagers from the village on the grounds of the ashram. Then, he began to recite the mantra in a loud voice and the villagers repeated the mantra after him.

Ramanand's guru then asked him, "What is all this?"

Ramanand replied, "Guru*ji*, I am getting the villagers to recite the mantra that you gave me."

The guru asked him, "Why did you do so?"

Ramanand answered, "You said that by chanting this mantra, one can attain heaven."

The guru said, "But I also said that if you disclose the mantra to anybody, you will incur sin and will go to hell."

Ramanand laughed and replied…

———————— **Pearls of Wisdom** ————————

1. What did Ramanand reply?

2. What is the moral of the story?

To gain pearls of wisdom, try to answer the questions on your own before referring to the answers given below.

Answers

1. Ramanand said, "Guru*ji*, if it is a question of hundreds of people attaining heaven, then I am ready to go to hell."

2. A person who only thinks about the good of others is not bothered by profit or loss, or good karma or sin. His only goal is the good of others and is ready to bear what comes his way with equanimity.

21

The Mystery of the Broken Trunk

Natarajan was a sculptor. He was a devotee of Lord Ganesh. Every year, lots of people would buy his idols during the various festivals like *Ganesh Chaturthi, Durga Pooja,* etc. Once during the Ganesh festival, the village headman commissioned him to make a sculpture of Lord Ganesh which would be ten feet tall. This was the first order of its kind for Natarajan and he was excited. His entire family was helping him in his work.

Natarajan completed the first mould of the statue and placed the idol against the wall which had a window at the top. He stood back and looked at the idol. Without meaning to, he felt proud of his craftsmanship. He locked the door of the room and went to bed.

The next morning, to his shock, he found that the trunk of Lord Ganesh was broken. It lay on the floor at a distance from the idol. He was horrified. He thought about what might have happened. Were the materials used of inferior quality? Was the mixture he had prepared too thick or too thin?

Without finding an answer, he got back to work again and completed the idol by night. Again, he locked the room and went to bed. But imagine his shock when the next morning he again found the trunk of the idol broken. Natarajan was in tears. He called his entire family and showed them what had happened. All of them were distressed.

"Your *Sadesati* (a period of 7.5 years when Saturn transits through a person's zodiac sign) is going on right now, son," said his mother, "better pray to Lord Hanuman to reduce its ill-effects." Accordingly, Natarajan prayed to Lord Hanuman. His son was watching this quietly.

Again, Natarajan fixed the trunk of Lord Ganesh. The next morning, once again he woke to find it broken. Now he was terribly distressed. His mother lamented, "O Shani Dev! Spare my child this torture and punish me for all his sins!" His wife silently prayed to Lord Krishna to help her husband.

Natarajan said, "O Ganesha! Why do you punish me so, my Lord? Is it because I was proud of how fine an idol I had made? Are you punishing me for my arrogance? Or is it that I have forgotten how to make sculptures? But no! I am sure of my craftsmanship and I know there is no mistake in the way I am sculpting your idol. Help me Lord!"

"Let us do a special puja today," said his mother. So a special puja was performed.

Natarajan's son was observing all this. In the evening he said, "Father, let us wait in the room tonight and watch what happens." Natarajan thought it was a brilliant idea. So after everybody had gone to sleep, Natarajan and his son crouched in the dark room with bated breath to see what happened.

At around 2 am, they heard a noise at the window and saw something enter through the window and jump on the trunk. The trunk broke into two. Natarajan and his son smiled happily at each other!

Pearls of Wisdom

1. What was the cause of the broken trunk? Why were Natarajan and his son smiling?

2. What is the moral of the story?

To gain pearls of wisdom, try to answer the questions on your own before referring to the answers given below.

Answers

1. The cause of the broken trunk was a cat. It was interested in the mouse below the Ganesh idol. It would enter through the window, jump on the trunk first and then jump to the floor, thus breaking the trunk. Natarajan realized that contrary to what he and his family thought, the gods were not angry with him and so he and his son smiled.

2. Some things that happen have a perfectly logical and rational explanation. It is up to us to decide whether to look at a problem rationally and solve it or become fearful and behave superstitiously.

22

Can God Do It?

Shravan was a hardworking businessman. His mother believed in God. She also prayed often for his success. As Shravan grew more and more successful, he became more and more arrogant.

Once his mother told him, "Shravan, you should thank God for helping you and making you successful." Immediately, Shravan replied, "What for, Mother? My success and my achievements are due to my efforts and my hard work. God had nothing to do with them."

"How can you say so?" asked his mother. "Whatever we get is God's gift to us. We must appreciate it."

Shravan said, "If God is so powerful, then I dare Him to kill me within the next five minutes." When nothing happened in the next five minutes, he laughed loudly and said, "See, I told you so."

His mother said nothing. A few hours later, his mother got into an argument with her young grandson. "Shravan," she shouted. "Your son is troubling me and calling me names," she said. Shravan admonished the child. "No! That's not enough," she said. "If you are a man, take this knife and kill him!"

Shravan was shocked. "What are you saying, Mother?" he asked.

"Oh! So you won't do it! Then accept that you are not a man!" said his mother.

Shravan said, "Mother, what are you saying? I am a man alright, but how can I kill my child to prove it?"

To that his mother said…

———————— **Pearls of Wisdom** ————————

    1. What did his mother say?

_____

To gain pearls of wisdom, try to answer the question on your own before referring to the answer given below.

Answer

1. His mother said, "It is the same with God. He is God and He is powerful but how can He kill His child to prove it?"

23

The Two Blessings of Krishna

Once, Krishna and Uddhav went out for a walk. After they had walked for a long time, they were quite tired. Then they saw a huge house before them. Krishna asked Uddhav to go to the house and ask the people for water. The head of the family made them welcome and served them water and refreshments. While leaving, Krishna blessed the man, saying that he would get more riches and live in greater luxury.

They went on their way. Again, after sometime, Krishna was thirsty. This time, they came across a small hut. It looked barren except for the presence of a cow. Uddhav went into the hut to ask for water. The door was opened by an ascetic. Regretfully, he told Uddhav that he had nothing to give them. But then he thought for a moment and said that he could give them milk from his beloved cow. He offered them the milk and told them that no matter what, he knew he could depend on his cow.

Krishna drank the milk. After they had left, Krishna raised his hand and blessing the man said, "O ascetic, may you be blessed! May your cow die soon!"

On hearing this, Uddhav was shocked. He wondered why Krishna had blessed the rich man who had lots to give him and had cursed the ascetic when he had given them the little that he had possessed. He thought it was very unfair.

But Krishna told him that he had indeed blessed the ascetic. He explained how...

———————————   **Pearls of Wisdom**   ———————————

1. What did Krishna tell Uddhav?

2. What is the moral of this story?

To gain pearls of wisdom, try to answer the questions on your own before referring to the answers given below.

Answers

1. Krishna told Uddhav that when He blessed people, he gave them what they needed rather than what they wanted. The ascetic was at a stage from where he could reach *mukti*. The only thing that separated him from the Ultimate Truth was his attachment to his cow. Once that attachment was broken, he would reach Him and so Krishna had 'blessed' the ascetic that his cow, his most beloved possession, would die.

2. Many times, when things don't go our way or when we don't get what we want, we feel that God is not with us or that He is not supporting us. But we must realize that God knows better and that He always gives us what is best for us, whether we understand it or not.

24

Lord Narayan and Tulsi

Tulsi was the wife of Jalandhar, the king of Asuras. Though Jalandhar was actually a *Shivansh* (a part of Lord Shiva), he had begun to tread on the wrong path, and out of arrogance, had vowed to destroy Lord Shiva.

Jalandhar's guru, Shukracharya, was worried for his safety. He told Tulsi to undertake special austerities. Once those austerities were completed, Jalandhar would be invincible. (It is believed that if a wife who is faithful and devoted to her husband undertakes austerities or a vow for his safety, she is rewarded for her commitment and devotion and her husband will be blessed with a long life).

Tulsi was a great devotee of Lord Narayan (Lord Vishnu). Many times, Jalandhar had told her to stop praying to Him, but her belief in Him would not be shaken.

As per Shukracharya's instruction, Tulsi carefully completed all the requirements. Now, only the last one remained where she and her husband would circumambulate Lord Narayan and she would apply the sacred *tika* on her husband's forehead. Then Jalandhar would be invincible.

Accordingly, Tulsi told Jalandhar that they would complete the last of the requirements. But just then, Jalandhar was called for a war. He told Tulsi to wait till he was back. He would make arrangements for the war and be back soon.

Tulsi waited for some time and soon Jalandhar appeared. As per Shrukracharya's instructions, both of them circumambulated the idol of Lord Narayan and Tulsi applied the sacred *tika* on her husband's forehead. As soon as she had touched him, she realized that the person before her was not her husband. Shocked, she asked the man who he was.

To her surprise, Lord Narayan revealed Himself. He had taken the form of Jalandhar and had completed the last rituals with her.

But since she had completed these austerities with someone other than her husband, the austerities had been disrupted and were of no use to protect her husband. Besides, she herself had been maligned.

Shocked by what had happened, she asked Lord Narayan, "O Narayan! All my life I have been a sincere devotee. Not even my husband's entreaties to stop praying to You could shake my belief in You. And when I am doing my duty as a wife, it is *You* who have come to disrupt the rituals and malign my name! How could You do this to the one who has only believed in You unconditionally? Please tell me where have I incurred sin? Was my devotion to You untrue?"

Lord Narayan said, "You devotion was true and pure. It is true that you have never incurred sin. Even while completing these rituals, you were only doing them out of pure devotion towards your husband and fulfilling your duty as a wife."

"Then why, O Narayan, did you do this?! I cannot go back to my husband as I am chaste no more. I do not wish to live any more.

I have decided to give up my life." Saying so, she cursed Lord Narayan that just as she had been maligned for no fault of hers, He too would have to take birth as a human and His wife too would have to undergo the same fate for no fault of hers.

Narayan said, "Since you are a faithful wife and a true devotee, I accept your curse. When the right time comes, I will be born as a human and my wife will undergo the same fate as yours and we too will suffer as you have suffered. For your devotion, from now on, people will only think of you as pure and holy and worship you before they worship me, and I shall bless whoever worships you. But then too Tulsi, I would like to explain to you that in whatever I have done, I was just doing my duty and had no other intention."

Tulsi was even more shocked to hear this, "How can you call this doing Your duty?"

—————   **Pearls of Wisdom**   —————

1. What did Lord Narayan answer?

2. What can we learn from this story?

To gain pearls of wisdom, try to answer the questions on your own before referring to the answers given below.

Answers

1. Lord Narayan answered, "I had no intention of harming you, O Tulsi. Whatever I did was only to protect the universe from Jalandhar. He is planning to destroy Lord Shiva Himself and

rule the universe. What he is doing is wrong. If you were to complete your austerities, Jalandhar would become invincible and cause harm to the universe. My duty is to protect the universe. So even if your devotion to me is true and your love for your husband is pure, I cannot allow him to succeed and become invincible. Even if it means incurring your wrath and getting cursed by you, so be it. I am duty-bound to protect the universe and shall accept whatever is the result of my action."

2. Lord Narayan's behaviour is an important lesson to us.

Firstly, He too was duty-bound by the laws of the universe and did whatever he had to do to ensure that the universe would be protected.

Secondly, God does not break laws of Nature for His own benefit or for the benefit of man. Everybody has to go through the law of Creation and Nature.

Thirdly, in order to fulfil His duty, Lord Narayan was also ready to incur Tulsi's wrath and was ready to live her curse. He rewarded her for her devotion and accepted His devotee's right to punish Him for what she thought was unfair.

Fourthly, if we do something which is against the laws of Nature or Creation, or against the good of mankind, we cannot expect God to help us to be successful.

25

Yudhisthir and the Dog

Yudhisthir, his brothers and their wife Draupadi had decided to go on their final pilgrimage. It was a pilgrimage up a difficult mountain path, which would lead to heaven. If one of them fell on the way, the others would have to leave him and continue ahead on their own paths.

Yudhisthir walked first, followed by Bheem, Arjun, Nakul, Sahadev and Draupadi. Somewhere along the way, a dog joined them on their journey.

Draupadi was the first to fall, followed by Sahadev, Nakul, Arjun and Bheem. Yudhisthir went ahead on his path, all alone. The dog followed him wherever he went.

When Yudhisthir reached the mountain peak, Lord Indra Himself came to take him to Heaven. As Yudhisthir sat in Indra's chariot, he insisted that the dog accompany them too.

Indra said, "That is impossible. A dog cannot enter Heaven. You must leave it here. You can enter Heaven due to your extraordinary qualities, but the same cannot be said of the dog."

Yudhisthir then calmly told Indra, "If my dog cannot accompany me to Heaven, I too shall not go. The dog has been faithful to me.

It loved me unconditionally. I cannot forsake it even for the sake of Heaven!"

Lord Indra was pleased with Yudhisthir's words and said, "O Yudhisthir! No other person in your place would have forsaken Heaven for a dog. You stand apart among all humans! The dog who followed you was the Lord of Dharma Himself who wanted to test you."

————————— **Pearls of Wisdom** —————————

1. What qualities of Yudhisthir can we notice from this story?

To gain pearls of wisdom, try to answer the question on your own before referring to the answer given below.

Answer

1. Through his behaviour, Yudhisthir showed great compassion for the dog. He was unfazed by the chance of entering Heaven. He had always believed in behaving righteously and with equanimity, and this time too, he did the same. Even at the possibility of having to forgo Heaven, he refused to leave the dog behind.

26

God's Plan

Surendra was a temple priest. He was a simpleton and was devoted to God. Hundreds of people would come to the temple daily, make offerings, chant prayers and ask God for something or the other. *How tired God must be of standing in one place listening to everybody,* he thought. One day, he spoke to God about it.

"God, if it is of any help to you, I am willing to stand in your place for a day so that you can take a break." God said, "Sure, that would be great. But just follow my instructions. Stand quietly just like I do. Don't be affected by what people do or say. Don't respond to them. Everything will work out as per my plan." Surendra happily agreed.

The next day, he was transformed into the idol of God and stood in His place in the temple. Very early in the morning, a rich woman came. She prayed for her husband's success and gave a huge donation. By mistake, she left her purse behind. Surendra saw her purse, but remembered that he could not call out to her.

She was followed by the flower seller of the temple, who took out a one rupee coin and prayed to the Lord for her family's survival. After finishing her prayers, she saw the purse full of money. Thinking that she had been gifted the purse by God Himself, she took it and went away. Surendra wanted to call her back, but he knew that he wasn't supposed to.

Then came an air hostess. She was supposed to go on a long flight and had come to pray for a safe journey. Meanwhile, the rich woman who had forgotten her purse came back to the temple with a policeman. Since the air hostess was standing at the spot where she had forgotten her purse, she told the police to arrest the air hostess on suspicion.

The air hostess was out of her wits. She appealed to God to prove her innocence and save her from the police. Surendra could remain silent no more and decided to use his powers as God. He spoke to the rich woman and cleared the misunderstanding by telling her that it was the flower seller of the temple who had innocently taken her purse and that the air hostess was indeed innocent. The rich woman said that she would find the flower seller and get her purse back.

They all thanked God for coming to their rescue and went away. At the end of the day, God asked Surendra how he had fared. "What you do is simply amazing, Lord," said Surendra. "But I too did something good today." He went on to narrate the story of the rich woman, the flower seller and the air hostess.

But God smiled subtly on hearing this. "I told you not to interfere with anything that was going on, didn't I? Everything was happening according to my plan. Do you know what the truth is?" asked God.

"No. Please tell me," said Surendra.

Then God told him the truth. Surendra was ashamed of himself.

--- **Pearls of Wisdom** ---

1. What was the truth?

2. What is the moral of this story?

To gain pearls of wisdom, try to answer the questions on your own before referring to the answers given below.

Answers

1. God told Surendra, "The money that the rich woman had donated had been accumulated by her husband by cheating people. She was offering that money to me and was asking for her husband's success. By losing her husband's money, the rich woman's bad karma would have been reduced a little.

   The poor flower seller deserved the purse. I wanted to reward her for her devotion and faith. She would have used it well and also given some money to those poorer than her.

   Had the air hostess been detained by the police due to a false accusation, she would actually have been saved because the plane she is going to board is supposed to crash. But now you have interfered with the plan."

2. Things are not what they seem all the time. Many times, we cannot comprehend God's plan behind what happens. But we must believe that nothing in this world goes unnoticed by Him and that He has a plan for everyone and everything.

27

The King and His Belief in God

There once lived a king who didn't believe in God. His Prime Minister was very unhappy about this. He tried to assure the King that there was a God who ruled the universe. The King in turn gave him various arguments. Finally he said, "Answer three questions I have about God satisfactorily, and I shall definitely believe in God. The three questions are:

1. Where is God?

2. Which way does He look?

3. What is the nature of His work?"

The minister went away depressed. He was sure that no one would be able to satisfactorily answer the King's questions. His young son was a bright boy who was blessed with knowledge. He asked the minister to allow him to answer the King's questions. Hesitatingly, the minister agreed.

On the appointed day, the boy went to the court to answer the questions instead of the minister. "Now we shall begin," said the King enthusiastically. The King asked his first question, "Where is God?"

The boy asked the attendants to get him a jug of milk. Then he asked the King to find butter in it. The King replied, "How can there be butter in the milk right now? It needs to be churned first to bring out the butter. Only then can it be seen separately."

The boy replied...

――――――――― **Pearls of Wisdom** ―――――――――

1. What did the boy reply?

_____

Next, the King asked the boy, "Which way does God look?"

The boy asked the attendants to open the windows so that sunlight could stream in. "Which way is the sunlight pointing, O King?"

"In no particular direction, but it lights up the whole room," said the King.

――――――――― **Pearls of Wisdom** ―――――――――

2. What did the boy reply?

_____

Satisfied, the King asked the third question: What is the nature of God's work?

The boy answered, "Bring me a cow." When a cow was brought in the court, the boy asked the King, "What is the colour of the cow?"

"Brown," he answered.

"And what is the colour of the grass it eats?"

"Green," he said.

"And what is the colour of the milk it gives?"

"White," he answered.

"Now tell me how old am I?" said the boy.

"Twelve," said the King.

"How old are you?" he asked the King.

"Fifty," he replied.

"So, a twelve-year-old boy is answering the queries raised by a fifty-year-old king! Now, can you tell me what God does?" asked the boy.

─────────────── **Pearls of Wisdom** ───────────────

3. What did the King answer?

_____

To gain pearls of wisdom, try to answer the questions on your own before referring to the answers given below.

Answers

1. The boy replied, "Just as the milk and the butter are one at present, God is one with the Universe. Just as milk needs to be churned to bring out the butter, the mind needs to be churned with true devotion and meditation in order to be able to see God. The best place to look for God is within ourselves."

2. The boy said, "Just like sunlight isn't limited to a particular direction, God's attention too is not limited to a particular direction. He sees the entire universe and even beyond. He sees the past, present and future too. He sees what we can see and also that which we are incapable of fathoming."

3. The King answered, "Everything that happens is what God does! It is His work that a brown cow eats green grass and gives white milk. He makes a twelve-year-old boy knowledgeable enough to teach a fifty-year-old King! This is nothing but the glory of God!"

STORIES

on

ISLAM

28

The Wonderful Ways of Allah

Aman was the sole survivor of a shipwreck. He had been washed up on a lonely island. A pious person at heart, he immediately prayed to Allah to save him.

Though he prayed fervently everyday, nothing seemed to be happening. Finally, he decided to collect wood from dead trees and build a hut for himself.

One day, when he came back after looking around for food, he found that his little hut that he had painstakingly built was in flames. He burst into tears as he saw the smoke devouring his hut rise up in the sky.

"Every day of my life I have prayed to you. I have lived my life as a good human being. Why then do you forsake me at the time I need you the most, O Allah?" he cried in despair.

When the sun rose the next morning, he heard the sound of a boat. He found that it was a lifeboat which had come to rescue him! It belonged to a ship which was nearby.

His joy knew no bounds! He asked his rescuers, "How did you know there was someone here?"

—————— **Pearls of Wisdom** ——————

1. What did his rescuers say?

2. What is the moral of this story?

To gain pearls of wisdom, try to answer the questions on your own before referring to the answers given below.

Answers

1. His rescuers answered, "We saw your smoke signal."

2. It is easy to lose faith in God when things are going wrong and do not seem to improve. But no matter what the circumstances, we must remember that Allah is helping us through His wonderful ways. Every single thing that happens in your life is the Mercy of Allah.

29

Be With Me, Allah!

Ruhee lived in a students' hostel in a big city. She was completing her graduation and was eager to go back to her town. One day, news of horrific crimes committed against women in her area were reported in the newspapers. The police were on the lookout for the man, but had no news of him yet.

Ruhee was quite tense and worried as she had joined a language class which finished quite late in the evening. There was no one who could accompany her to her class and be with her until she reached the hostel safely. She prayed to Allah to keep her safe.

One evening, her class had finished particularly late and she was walking back to her hostel when it began to rain and the street lights went off. She was scared and started running. She came across a small stretch of road which she had to cross before she could reach the main road. There she saw a tall man standing alone. There were only the two of them on that road.

She called out to Allah for help. "Please be with me, Allah. Please help me to safety," she prayed desperately. Her inner voice told her to keep walking steadily. She did so and soon passed the man and came to the main road. She thanked Allah as she reached her hostel.

The very next day, the papers reported that the previous night, a girl had been badly assaulted on the same road which Ruhee had passed and the police had caught a man they suspected of the crime. The crime had been committed around the same time too. This shocked Ruhee and she went to the police station and told them that she had passed through the same lane yesterday and could probably identify the man. The police said that she could see him but the man had already confessed to the crime. When she was taken to see him, she saw that it was the same man whom she had passed the small road.

I could have been the victim, she thought. She was then curious as to why had he not attacked her when she had passed by the same road, at around the same time. She asked him the reason.

The man replied...

---------------------- **Pearls of Wisdom** ----------------------

1. What did the man reply?

2. What can we learn from this story?

To gain pearls of wisdom, try to answer the questions on your own before referring to the answers given below.

Answers

1. The man replied that he had seen her walking with a well-built man and so he had not attacked her.

2. Ruhee had called Allah to help her overcome the dangerous situation. He came to her rescue and the criminal thought that there was someone with her and left her alone. Allah is merciful and He always protects those who ask Him for help.

30

The Sick Man

A traveller from a desert once saw a blind man on his travels. The old man was sick, his body was full of sores and he seemed to be in pain. But Allah's name was constantly on his lips. He would say, "Allah is Merciful! He loves me and helps me be healthy and happy."

The traveller was stunned. "But you seem so ill, sir. It is difficult for you to move. The sores give you pain and you cannot see. What then are you thankful for?"

―――――――――― **Pearls of Wisdom** ――――――――――

    1. What did the old man say?

    2. What is the moral of the story?

To gain pearls of wisdom, try to answer the questions on your own before referring to the answers given below.

Answers

1. The old man said, "Why? There is nothing wrong with me! I am able to take His name with my lips, thank Him for

everything He has given me and I am aware of His presence in my life. What more does a man require?"

2. Truly, taking God's name, being thankful for what we have, and knowing that He is with us, is the true essence of a life well lived.

31

The Grapes

Prophet Muhammad would share the gifts he got with others. One day, a poor man brought grapes for him.

But on that day, Prophet Muhammad did not share the grapes with anyone else and ate them all by himself.

Pearls of Wisdom

1. Why did the Prophet Muhammad not share the grapes with anyone that day?

To gain pearls of wisdom, try to answer the question on your own before referring to the answer given below.

Answer

1. The grapes were sour, so Prophet Muhammad did not share them. He did not want to hurt the man's feelings by pointing it out as the man had gifted the grapes with love.

32

For Allah Only

Some people once told a pious man that a group of people were worshipping a tree. He decided to cut down the tree and picked up his axe to do so.

But the devil took the form of a man, came to him and asked him what he was doing. The man said he was going to cut the tree. Then, to distract him, the devil said that had God really wanted that to happen, he would have told his prophets to do it. There was no need for the man to interfere.

They both argued against one another, when finally they came to physical blows and the man knocked down the devil. Then the devil begged forgiveness and said, "Let us make a deal. Leave this tree as it is until you receive God's command to cut it. I shall pay you two gold coins daily. You can keep one for yourself and give one to the poor."

The man was tempted and gave in to the devil. The next morning, he saw two gold coins under his pillow. He kept one gold coin for himself and gave one to the poor. But the next day, he didn't see the coins. He decided to cut the tree and went to it with his axe.

Again, the devil came there in the form of an old man. He told the man that he shouldn't cut the tree and the man refused. Again, they came to physical blows. But this time, the devil knocked down the man.

The man wondered how he had lost to the devil this time when he had won the last time. Then he realized...

───────────── **Pearls of Wisdom** ─────────────

1. What did the man realize?

To gain pearls of wisdom, try to answer the question on your own before referring to the answer given below.

Answer

1. The man realized that no one can defeat someone who is doing something for the love of Allah. But he who does something only for his own material gain, is defeated. The first time, he won because his *intention* of cutting the tree was to do something for Allah. But after receiving the coins, his intention turned monetary. God's spiritual strength which he had received on the first day had disappeared on the second day.

33

Prophet Idris

Prophet Idris was born and brought up in Babylon. He was the fifth generation of Prophet Adam. He counseled people to return to the religion of their forefathers. But only a few people listened to him. In spite of this, he continued to preach the message of Allah.

One day, Prophet Idris told his followers, "I am quite weary of living in Babylon. People here do not worship Allah and instead worship idols. Let us go where we can worship Allah alone and where people will accept Allah's message and join us in His worship."

One of his disciples asked him, "But will we be able to find a place as fertile as Babylon?"

────────── **Pearls of Wisdom** ──────────

1. What did Prophet Idris reply?

2. What is the moral of the story?

To gain pearls of wisdom, try to answer the questions on your own before referring to the answers given below.

Answers

1. Prophet Idris replied, "Do not worry. We are migrating for the love of Allah, so be assured that He will never forsake us. Wherever we go, He will definitely give us our food."

2. If your intentions are purely for the sake of Allah, be assured that no matter what happens, He will never forget you. You will always be helped and protected by Him.

34

Prophet Ibrahim and His Dream

Once, Prophet Ibrahim had a dream that he was slaughtering his son, Ismail. His son was a young man by then. The dream made Prophet Ibrahim sad as he was sure that this was Allah's message to him. He told his son, "Son, I had a dream where I was offering you as a sacrifice to Allah."

Ismail said, "Father, please obey the order that Allah has given you through the dream." He added, "O Father, put me upside down on the ground so that you will not be able to see my face and your emotions will not get the better of you and your hand will not falter." Prophet Ibrahim accordingly lay his son on the ground and took up his knife to sacrifice him. He had just put his knife on his son's neck when he heard a voice which said, "Ibrahim, do not sacrifice your son. Instead, take this sheep and sacrifice it."

Prophet Ibrahim saw a sheep nearby and sacrificed it instead of his son.

————————— **Pearls of Wisdom** —————————

1. Why did Prophet Ibrahim have the dream of sacrificing his son?

2. Why was his son saved?

To gain pearls of wisdom, try to answer the questions on your own before referring to the answers given below.

Answers

1 & 2. Prophet Ibrahim saw the dream and understood that it was Allah's message to him. The dream was meant to test him. However, he had complete faith in Allah and successfully passed the test and thus, his son was saved.

35

Prophet Ayub

Prophet Ayub was a wealthy man. However, his wealth had not led him to become arrogant and he was always thankful to Allah for everything he had. He also helped people who came to him.

Once, Allah decided to test him. He took away everything that Prophet Ayub had, including his wealth and children. Additionally, he was also afflicted with a skin disease. His entire body, except for his tongue, was affected. But it did not affect his faith in Allah and he kept thanking and remembering Allah every day.

Eventually, everyone was sick and tired of serving him and began to leave him and go away. Only his wife remained dutiful and served him to the best of her ability. She even had to work in other houses for a living.

Prophet Ayub bore his disease patiently for 18 years. He did not complain. He sincerely prayed to Allah for his health to be restored. He begged Allah for His mercy.

Allah finally accepted his prayer. He told him to hit the ground with his foot. Immediately, a fountain of cold, sweet water came up. Allah told him to bathe in the water and drink it. Once he bathed in the water and drank it, Prophet Ayub recovered from his illness completely.

Pearls of Wisdom

1. What is the moral of this story?

It had so happened that during the time he was ill, he had once called out to his wife. But she didn't come immediately. Prophet Ayub was angered by this and swore that when he got better, he would punish his wife with 100 lashes. But now that he was healed, he thought that if he didn't keep his word, he would incur sin and if he did, he would hurt his loving and dutiful wife.

Once again, he asked Allah what he should do. Allah told him to keep his promise by hitting his wife once with a broom made up of 100 straws. This way Allah kept up Prophet Ayub's word without him hurting his wife.

Pearls of Wisdom

2. Why did Allah allow Prophet Ayub to keep his promise by hitting his wife only once?

To gain pearls of wisdom, try to answer the questions on your own before referring to the answers given below.

Answers

1. Allah is merciful. When Prophet Ayub was afflicted with the disease, he only asked Allah for help. He knew that only Allah could heal him from his disease. He continuously prayed to Allah all throughout his disease. He was a patient man and

passed Allah's test. Similarly, no matter how difficult things become, we too should have complete faith that Allah will help us to overcome our difficulties.

2. Prophet Ayub's wife was devoted to him. In spite of everybody leaving him, she stayed with him and nursed him to the best of her ability. Both he and his wife had passed Allah's test with flying colours. So Allah allowed him to hit his wife only once and keep his promise.

36

Prophet Dawood and His Lesson on Justice

The people of Bani Israel were at war against the Palestinians. The chief of the Palestinian army was Jaloot. He was a non-believer and was extremely courageous and powerful. None of the people of Bani Israel were ready to face Jaloot.

Jaloot on the other hand was aware of this. He rode into the battlefield brandishing his sword and challenged them saying, "Isn't there anyone who is capable of facing me?"

Dawood was an ordinary man in the battalion of Bani Israel. He courageously came ahead to fight Jaloot. He was armed only with a catapult. He placed a stone in the catapult, aimed it right at Jaloot's forehead and hit him in such a way that Jaloot fell to the ground. Then Dawood sat on Jaloot's chest, drew his sword and beheaded him.

Dawood was made the king of Bani Israel and Allah also made him a prophet. Allah decided to teach people about justice through Prophet Dawood. Once, when he was praying in his house, two men entered it by jumping over a wall.

The two men said, "We have come to ask you for justice." Then, one of the men said that his friend who was with him owned 99 ewes while he owned just one. Now his friend was asking him for that one ewe as well so that he could own 100 ewes.

Without waiting for the other friend to speak, Prophet Dawood said, "A friend who says so does an injustice to his friend. A good friend cannot act unjustly towards his own friend."

Immediately, the two men disappeared. Prophet Dawood realized his mistake.

Pearls of Wisdom

1. What was Prophet Dawood's mistake?

2. Who were the two people?

To gain pearls of wisdom, try to answer the questions on your own before referring to the answers given below.

Answers

1 & 2. The two people were angels who had been sent by Allah to teach Prophet Dawood to do justice. Prophet Dawood's mistake was that he had not patiently listened to the second man's side before giving his decision. He had reacted after hearing only one man's side. A king has to hear both sides carefully before coming to a decision.

37

God Gives Us Our Food

Hamid was walking through the jungle. He heard a noise and went and hid behind a tree. He was surprised to see a jackal without any limbs. He wondered, "O God! How will this jackal get its food? How will it survive in the jungle without a limb?" He decided to wait and see what happened.

Soon, he saw a lioness come there with a small deer in her mouth. She ate the deer and the leftovers remained on the ground. After she had left, the jackal stealthily crept up to the carcass and began to eat its fill. After eating, it limped back into the bushes.

"Wonderful! So God provides food to each and every one of His beings," thought Hamid. "Wonderful are His ways! Just as He provides food to the jackal, He will provide me with food too."

The next day, instead of going for work and earning his bread, he went to the mosque and sat on the ground outside it, waiting for his food to come to him. People came and went and looked at him curiously. Hamid waited patiently for God to give him his food. But no one even asked him who he was or what he wanted.

By evening he was very hungry and thirsty. In a weak voice he asked God, "O God! I am hungry and thirsty. When are you going to give me my food?"

———————— **Pearls of Wisdom** ————————

1. What did God answer?

To gain pearls of wisdom, try to answer the question on your own before referring to the answer given below.

Answer

1. God said, "Hamid, even animals make their own efforts and hunt for food. You are a human being. You have been blessed with hands and legs and intelligence too. How can you receive food unless you work for it? Remember, God helps those who help themselves!"

38

Syedna Hazrat Ibrahim

As a child, Syedna Hazrat Ibrahim's father would ask him to sell idols. But Syedna Hazrat Ibrahim was a true believer in Allah. He would ask his father, "Why do you worship idols which cannot respond to you? Listen to what I am telling you, for I am knowledgeable about faith. Do not worship idols."

But in spite of all this, his father refused to listen to him. Syedna Hazrat Ibrahim preached Allah's message to the people as well. But they simply did not listen to him and kept on worshipping idols. He decided that he would now have to prove to them that the idols were only stones which couldn't respond or help them.

One day, his people had gone to a fair nearby. Syedna Hazrat Ibrahim went to the biggest temple. Here, all statues were placed in an orderly manner. At the highest spot, the biggest one among them had been placed and before it were placed many offerings. Syedna Hazrat Ibrahim asked the idols why they weren't eating the offerings. When he got no reply, he asked them why they weren't responding to him. But again he got no reply.

Then he took his axe and began to break all the idols except for the biggest idol. After he had broken the remaining idols, he placed his axe in the hands of the biggest idol.

When people returned from the fair, they saw what had happened to all the idols. They looked for the culprit. Then someone said, "Ibrahim always talks against our Gods. It must be him."

They complained about this to the King who ordered that Hazrat Ibrahim should be caught and presented before him. The King asked him whether it was he who had broken the idols. Syedna Hazrat Ibrahim replied, "Why don't you ask the idols themselves?" The King said that he obviously couldn't ask the idols because they couldn't reply.

Then Syedna Hazrat Ibrahim said, "What a pity! You are praying to idols who can do you no good or bad, and who can't even respond to you and cannot even save themselves!"

No one including the King could argue with him, but to appease his anger, he ordered that Syedna Hazrat Ibrahim would be burnt alive. People gathered wood and a fire was lit. Everyone had come to see Syedna Hazrat Ibrahim being punished. They placed him in a canon so that he could be thrown into the fire.

But Syedna Hazrat Ibrahim was praying to Allah. He had complete faith that Allah would save him. He was thrown into the red, hot fire. People waited for the fire to die down. They wanted to ensure that Syedna Hazrat Ibrahim had indeed been killed.

────────────   **Pearls of Wisdom**   ────────────

1. What happened next?

2. What can we learn from this story?

To gain pearls of wisdom, try to answer the questions on your own before referring to the answers given below.

Answers

1. While Syedna Hazrat Ibrahim was in the fire, Allah ordered the fire to become cool, and thus saved him. The people were surprised to see that Syedna Hazrat Ibrahim was safe in spite of being thrown into the fire.

2. To get people to do the right things, a lot of courage and patience is needed. Syedna Hazrat Ibrahim was a courageous person. In spite of the circumstances he was in and the extreme opposition he was facing, he had complete faith in Allah.

STORIES

on

CHRISTIANITY

39

Where Are You, God?

Lilly was a very pious woman. She prayed to God every day. One day, after her prayers, she thought for a long time and said, "O God, all my life, I have lived as you have directed me to. I have been a good human being and have done my best. But today, I want to ask you for something. If I have truly done my duty, I want you to grant me a favour."

The Lord answered, "Ask and it shall be yours!"

Lilly said, "Lord, I wish you to see you with my own eyes."

The Lord replied, "I promise you that I shall pay you a visit tomorrow. Be ready for my visit."

Lilly had never been so happy in her life. The next day, she painstakingly cleaned and decorated her house and prepared the most delicious food to welcome the Lord to her humble home.

While she was preparing food, she heard a knock at her door. She rushed to open the door and found that it was the newspaper vendor. "Go away! Come back later. I have important visitors today," she shouted.

After she had finished her chores and sat waiting for God, again someone knocked at the door. Expecting God, she opened it with a huge smile on her face. But to her disappointment, it was her next door neighbor. "Sorry, I am busy today," she said and shooed her off.

Next came her friend whom she similarly sent off. She then sat waiting for hours expecting God to come in any minute. Minutes and hours passed, but there was no sign of Him. By evening, Lilly was close to tears. "How can God not keep His promise?" she thought.

The next morning, during her prayers, with tears in her eyes she asked Him, "Why didn't you fulfill your promise to me, O Lord?"

"But I did Lilly," said He. "I came to meet you not once, not twice but thrice. And each time, you asked me to leave."

"When did you come to meet me, Lord?" she asked.

He answered, "Try and recall who came to visit you yesterday."

She answered surprised, "But they were the newspaper vendor, my neighbour and my friend! When did you come?"

—————————— **Pearls of Wisdom** ——————————

1. What did the Lord say?

2. What can we learn from this story?

To gain pearls of wisdom, try to answer these questions on your own before referring to the answers given below.

Answers

1. God explained, "In spite of your true devotion, do you not know that I am present everywhere and in everyone? It was me all the three times. I changed my form because each time, you sent me off."

2. Lilly had made the same mistake that all of us do. In spite of our devotion, we refuse to believe that God is present everywhere and in everyone around us. Instead of respecting and loving His presence in our fellow creatures, we disrespect them and still expect God to meet us and bless us.

40

The Value of Life

A man once asked God, "What is the value of life?" God smiled and said, "It's a very difficult question. But you can try and find out for yourself. Here, take this stone. Show it to various people and ask them what they feel its value is but don't sell it."

The man first went to a grocer and asked him, "What according to you is the value of this stone?" The grocer looked at the stone keenly and said, "Looks useless to me. Throw it away!" The man thanked him and went on ahead.

Next, he went to a book seller. The book seller looked at the stone and said, "I'll give you a dozen of my comic books for it." The man thanked him and went away.

Then he went to an antique seller. The antique seller studied the stone for a long time and said, "I'll give you a priceless gem in exchange for this lovely stone." The man went ahead on his mission.

Next, he went to a shop which dealt in precious stones. The owner jumped in joy on seeing the stone. "I am so fortunate that you, sir, have brought this stone to me! Nothing I have can compensate you for this precious stone!"

Observing so many different reactions, the man was thoroughly confused and went back to God and narrated his experiences. "O Lord! I am confused," he said. "Please tell me what the value of life is."

Pearls of Wisdom

1. What does God reply?

2. What is the moral of this story?

To gain pearls of wisdom, try to answer these questions on your own before referring to the answers given below.

Answers

1. God told the man, "From the reactions of the grocer, book seller, antique seller and seller of precious stones, you can understand that no matter what you are, people will value you based on their outlook, their background, their awareness, their motives, their beliefs and their intentions. Life is precious, but the value of each one's life is thus different for different people."

2. No matter what value people assign to you, remember that it has nothing to do with your value. Do not get disheartened or feel threatened if someone doesn't have a good opinion about you. You are precious in the eyes of God! God made you and He doesn't do poor work!

41

Know What You Need

Bartimeaus was a beggar who lived on the road. He had no relatives, no food, no clothing and no shelter. Additionally, he was blind too.

One day, he met Jesus. Jesus asked him what he wished for.

There were many things that Bartimeaus required. He replied...

--------- *Pearls of Wisdom* ---------

1. What did Bartimeaus ask Jesus for?

2. What is the moral of this story?

To gain pearls of wisdom, try to answer these questions on your own before referring to the answers given below.

Answers

1. Bartimeaus asked Jesus for the one thing which was the most important among all his other needs and which would take care of all the rest of his needs. He asked Jesus for his sight.

2. Needs and wants are many and they keep changing over time. To achieve what one wants, one must be sure and ask specifically for what one wants to receive. Being sure lends power to your prayer. Additionally, man should not be dependent on the Lord alone. Bartimeaus asked Jesus for his sight so that once he was able to see, he would work and himself achieve the rest of the things that he needed.

42

Trust in God

A family of five were very poor. The four children lived with their widowed mother, Martha. They could barely make ends meet and at times even went hungry. One night, Martha realized she had nothing to give her children the next day.

She felt so helpless that she couldn't even ensure their survival. But she was a great believer in God and called out to Him. "Help me, God! Help our family to survive," she said.

By morning, nothing had happened. But she did not lose faith in the Lord. She prayed to Him once more to help her. Soon, her children woke and it was time for them to go to school.

"But we're hungry, Mother," said the youngest. Without losing faith in the Lord she responded, "Yes dear. Pray to the Lord and ask Him for food. Have faith in Him, for very soon He shall give us our food."

The children left for school. On their way, they passed by a church. The eldest took them in and they knelt down and prayed aloud to God. "O God, we have no food to eat and we are very hungry. Please help us. Please give our family some food so that we may be able to live."

After praying, they went on to school. On returning home, they saw a table loaded with fruits, bread, cake, eggs and everything they could possibly wish for. "Look," said the youngest, "God listened to our prayers and gave us so much food!"

"Who gave us the food, Mother?" asked the eldest. Martha replied with tears in her eyes, "It was your friend's mother. She heard you in the church and immediately came to our help. God has sent His angel to help us! Thank You, God!"

Pearls of Wisdom

1. What can we learn from this story?

To gain pearls of wisdom, try to answer the question on your own before referring to the answer given below.

Answer

1. Martha had immense faith in the Lord. She knew that no matter how bad the situation seemed, she could always count on the Lord for help to fulfil her needs. The Lord Himself has said, 'Ask and it shall be given unto you'. Be assured that you are always loved and protected by the Lord. Have faith in Him.

43

Jesus and Zacchaeus

Zacchaeus was a rich man. By profession he was a tax collector. Although he was supposed to deposit the money he collected with the Government, he often kept quite a bit for himself.

One day, when Jesus was travelling through Jericho, Zacchaeus came to see Him. But since he was quite short and there were many tall people around Jesus, Zacchaeus couldn't see Him. So he climbed a tree.

However, imagine his surprise when Jesus looked at him in the tree. Jesus told him that He wanted to go to Zacchaeus's house for food. Zacchaeus was very happy to hear this.

But the other people were not happy on hearing this. They did not want Jesus to go to Zacchaeus's house because he was dishonest.

But Jesus said…

———————— **Pearls of Wisdom** ————————

1. What did Jesus say?

To gain pearls of wisdom, try to answer the question on your own before referring to the answer given below.

Answer

1. Jesus told the people that He had come to save people who were sinners. He had come to find people who were sinners and who would let Him save them. Thus, He had to go to Zacchaeus's house.

44

Daniel and the Lions

Once upon a time, King Darius ruled Babylon. He was a wise king and had chosen people to help him in the administration. A man called Daniel was the leader of these men. But the men were not happy with Daniel being their leader.

Daniel was devoted to God. The evil men decide to go against Daniel. They went to the King and asked him to make a law by which people would not be allowed to pray to God. Those who would not obey this law would be punished. They would be put into the lion's cage.

Unperturbed by this law, Daniel prayed to God thrice a day. The evil men told the King about this. They asked for Daniel to be punished by enforcing the law.

The King was completely against this, but he knew that the law could not be changed for one person. So he gave orders for Daniel to be put into the lion's cage. But the King went and spoke to Daniel. He said, "God will save you."

The King decided to fast and pray for Daniel's safety. He couldn't sleep all night due to anxiety.

In the morning, he rushed to the lion's cage to look for Daniel.

Pearls of Wisdom

1. What do you think had happened to Daniel?

2. What is the moral of this story?

To gain pearls of wisdom, try to answer the questions on your own before referring to the answers given below.

Answers

1. Daniel was alive and well. The lion hadn't hurt him.

2. In spite of the law made by the King, Daniel prayed to God regularly. God always helps those who believe in Him completely.

45

Elijah and the Priests of Baal

This story is about the wicked priests in Israel who worshipped an idol called Baal. Prophet Elijah wanted people to worship God. He asked King Ahab to bring all the people and the wicked priests of Baal to a mountain.

Prophet Elijah explained to the people that it was wicked to worship idols. They must choose to worship either God or Baal. He wanted people to understand that idols do not have power.

To prove this, he asked for two bulls and some wood for a sacrifice. Out of these, he gave one bull and some wood to the priests and kept one bull and some wood for himself. He then asked the priests not to ignite the fire for the sacrifice, but instead, pray to their idol Baal to ignite the sacrifice.

The evil priests prayed to Baal the entire morning. When nothing happened, they even jumped up on the altar and shouted to Baal. But Baal was just an idol. There was no reply from him. The priests prayed louder and harder but no matter how hard they prayed, the sacrifice was not ignited.

Then Elijah told the people that he would pray to God. God would send down the fire required for the sacrifice. Elijah built his altar and put the bull and wood on it. He asked some men for four barrels of water. He told them to pour the water on the sacrifice. Twice again, he asked the men to bring him four barrels of water and pour it on the sacrifice. Then Elijah prayed to God. He asked God to help him and ignite the sacrifice.

Pearls of Wisdom

1. What happened next?

2. What is the moral of this story?

To gain pearls of wisdom, try to answer the questions on your own before referring to the answers given below.

Answers

1. God responded to Elijah's prayer by sending down fire. The fire soaked up all the water and also burnt the wet wood.

2. Elijah wanted people to worship God. By doing all this, he proved to the people that idols had no power. He showed them the power of God.

46

David and Goliath

War was going on between the Philistines and the Israelites. Among the Philistines was a giant called Goliath. Needless to say, he was huge and strong. He knew that the Israelites were afraid of him.

One day he challenged them to send him a man to fight with him. But no one came. For forty days and forty nights, Goliath called out to them but none of the Israelites was ready to take up the challenge.

Jesse's sons were fighting in the Israelite army. When his son David went to give them some food, he saw Goliath. He heard him shouting and challenging the Israelites. He understood that nobody was willing to fight Goliath. He decided that he would fight Goliath himself.

This angered his brothers who felt that he should just take care of the sheep like he usually did. But David was unperturbed. He equipped himself with a sling and five stones and went to fight Goliath.

When Goliath saw David, he was surprised. He rebuked him. But David did not lose heart. He shouted at Goliath to begin the war.

Goliath attacked David. David immediately drew his sling, put in a stone and took a shot at Golaith. Bang! Goliath was hit right in the head and he fell. Taking advantage of this, David grabbed Goliath's sword and cut off his head. Seeing that the giant Goliath was dead, the Philistines were scared and took to their heels.

Pearls of Wisdom

1. How was David confident that he would be able to kill Goliath when nobody else was willing to face him?

2. What can we learn from this story?

To gain pearls of wisdom, try to answer the questions on your own before referring to the answers given below.

Answers

1. David believed in God. He knew that God would help him to kill Goliath and thus, he was successful where others were too afraid to try.

2. No matter what our shortcomings, and the magnitude of the challenges before us, if we truly believe that God will help us, we can achieve the seemingly impossible. All we have to do is believe.

47

Abraham and Issac

Abraham and his wife Sarah were righteous and regularly prayed to God. But they had only one sorrow. They had no children. When Sarah was 90 years old, God blessed Sara that she would have a son. Though she was too old to have a baby, she gave birth to a son and called him Issac. God said that Issac would be devoted to Him and would obey Him.

The birth of their son made the couple very happy and they loved their son dearly. God wanted to test Abraham. He told Abraham to take Issac to a mountain and sacrifice him. Abraham was very sad and did not want to sacrifice his son as he loved him dearly, but he also wanted to obey God.

Abraham and Issac travelled for three days and came to the mountain. Abraham carried a knife and Issac had some wood in his hands. They climbed up the mountain. Abraham prepared an altar and placed the wood on it. Then, he put Issac on the altar. He was about to sacrifice Issac when an angel appeared and stopped him and told him not to do so.

Then Abraham saw a ram in the bushes and knew that God had sent him the ram for the sacrifice. He then sacrificed the ram.

Pearls of Wisdom

1. Why was Abraham ready to sacrifice his son when he loved him dearly?

2. What can we learn from this story?

To gain pearls of wisdom, try to answer the questions on your own before referring to the answers given below.

Answers

1. Abraham loved his son but he also had complete faith in God. He knew that even though he had not understood the reason behind God's command, he had faith that God would only tell him to do something that was right.

2. Abraham's love of God and his faith in Him was much stronger than his love for his beloved son. We should learn to love and trust God the same way and serve Him as per His commands, even though we do not understand His ways.

48

Jesus and the Woman Who Had Sinned

As Jesus became more and more popular, the Pharisees began to hate Him. They tried to find fault with Him. Once, they decided to trap Him in public.

They brought a woman who had sinned to Jesus. Jesus was known for his forgiveness. The men were hoping that Jesus would forgive the woman so that they could find fault with Him and declare that He had disobeyed God's law.

They told Jesus that the woman was of a bad character and that she had been caught while committing adultery. By law, she had to be stoned to death, they said.

They then asked Him for His decision. On hearing this, Jesus said nothing but bent down and wrote something on the ground with His finger.

"Why do you keep mum?" the people demanded.

Then Jesus said…

The people were ashamed of themselves and left.

——————————— **Pearls of Wisdom** ———————————

1. What did Jesus say to the men?

2. Why did the men leave? What can we learn from this story?

To gain pearls of wisdom, try to answer the questions on your own before referring to the answers given below.

Answers

1. Jesus said, "The first one to throw a stone at this woman should be the one who has not sinned a single time."

2. The men realized that there was none amongst them who had never sinned a single time. Before pointing out the sins of others, we need to examine ourselves carefully. A person who is a sinner himself has no right to hurl accusations at and punish others.

49

Balaam and his Donkey
(Old Testament)

Balaam had saddled his donkey and was on his way to Balak. But the Lord was angry with him because Balaam was going to Balak for his own purposes and not for those of the Lord.

The Lord sent His angel with a sword to bar Balaam's way. Balaam did not see the Lord's angel, but his donkey did and it turned off the path. But Balaam hit it to bring it back to the road.

Next, the angel with the sword stood where there was a very narrow path having walls on both the sides. When the donkey saw the angel, once again it pressed close to the wall to avoid the angel. But Balaam's foot was crushed against the wall and he hit the donkey again.

The next time, the Lord's angel stood with the sword in such a place from where it was impossible to either turn left or right. When the donkey saw the angel before it, it lay down on the path. Balaam was now really furious and hit the donkey hard once more.

Then the donkey opened its mouth and asked Balaam, "What have I done for you to beat me thrice?"

Balaam told the donkey that he was so angry with its behaviour that had he a sword, he would have gladly killed the donkey then and there. Then the donkey asked him, "Do you ever remember me behaving in this way?"

When Balaam accepted that indeed the donkey had never behaved that way before, the Lord opened Balaam's eyes. It was then that he saw the Lord's angel with a sword. The angel asked him, "Why did you beat your donkey? It was I who blocked your path because it is not the path of the Lord. Your donkey saw me and turned off the path thrice. Otherwise, I would have killed you."

Balaam accepted that he had sinned and hadn't known that Lord had sent His angel to stop him. He told the angel that if the angel wished, he would go back immediately. The angel told Balaam that he could go ahead on the condition that he would speak only the words that the Lord put into his mouth and not his own words.

———————— **Pearls of Wisdom** ————————

1. How was it possible for Balaam's donkey to speak to him?

To gain pearls of wisdom, try to answer the question on your own before referring to the answer given below.

Answer

1. The Lord can use even a mere donkey to communicate His message to us.

50

Job and God

Job was a righteous man who obeyed God's commandments. God had blessed him with riches, a loving wife and ten children.

Satan was aware that Job was indeed honourable but he thought it was because God had blessed him. But what if Job's blessings were to be taken away?

However, God told Satan that Job would be righteous even if all he owned was taken away. Accordingly, one day, Job lost everything he owned – his animals, his farm, his house and was left with nothing. Even his children were killed.

But that made no difference to Job. He knew that he had had nothing when he was born; God had given him everything he had owned and now had taken it away. He still worshipped God as he had earlier.

God told Satan that taking away everything had made no difference to Job. Satan replied that if Job were to fall ill, he would no longer be righteous. Job became very ill and was in great pain. But still he didn't lose faith in God. He told his friends that he might die, but would still love God no matter what.

God then asked Job various questions which he answered to the best of his abilities. Then Job saw God. God blessed Job with much more than he had given him earlier.

Pearls of Wisdom

1. How was Job able to keep his faith in God in spite losing
   everything he had?

---

*To gain pearls of wisdom, try to answer the question on your own
before referring to the answer given below.*

Answer

1. Job knew that God Always Knows Best! Many times we don't
   understand why God does some things. But no doubt, there
   are strong reasons for everything that God does. All we can do
   is to have faith in Him.

51

The Spider and King David

As a young boy, David used to take care of his father's sheep. Often, while taking his sheep to graze, he would see many spiders. Their silken webs shone in the sun and he watched them with fascination. But David being an inquisitive boy wondered of what use spiders were.

Since he couldn't find the answer himself, he asked God his question. "Lord, what is the need for the world to have spiders?"

The Lord said, "O David! You will only realize this when one day you will need their help!"

David was a brave lad who was devoted to God. Keeping faith in God, he had defeated the massive giant Goliath. Then he got married to the daughter of King Saul. The people held David in high esteem.

But this did not go down well with King Saul. He felt bitter and threatened by David. He ordered his soldiers to kill David. Knowing that the soldiers were out to kill him, David ran away into the forests. The soldiers followed him and came very close to where he was.

Then David saw a cave. He ran inside the cave. But he knew that the soldiers would surely check for him in the cave. He didn't know what to do.

Then he saw a spider spinning a web across the mouth of the cave. It had just finished spinning the web when the soldiers came across it.

The soldiers looked at the cave and went away.

────────── **Pearls of Wisdom** ──────────

1. Why did the soldiers not go into the cave?

2. What is the moral of the story?

To gain pearls of wisdom, try to answer the questions on your own before referring to the answers given below.

Answers

1. The soldiers saw that the web was not broken. They thought that had David gone inside the cave, obviously, it would have been broken and so they left without looking for him in the cave.

2. Each creature on the Earth, no matter how small, is important and plays its own role in God's plan.

52

Tom and the Gold Coin

Harry was a pious man. He was kind to everybody around him. He owned a huge house and had many servants.

One of his servants, Tom, was very hot tempered. He would shout at others when he got angry and use bad words too. Harry often told Tom that God would not be happy with his behaviour. God wanted humans to be kind to each other and treat each other with love and respect.

But his saying so made no difference to Tom. He thought it was fine that God wanted him to be nice to people, but people were always out to get him and he had every right to get angry.

One day, Harry told him, "Tom, here is a gold coin. I will give it to you if you control your temper the entire day and do not say a single bad word to anyone." Of course, Tom agreed.

The same day, however, another servant accused Tom of not doing his work properly. Tom was just going to give it back to him when he remembered the gold coin and kept quiet. No matter who troubled him that day, Tom kept a tight control on his temper.

In the evening, he went to Harry and asked him for the gold coin. As promised, Harry gave him the coin. Then he said, "It's a shame!"

Pearls of Wisdom

1. What was a shame? Why was Harry not happy even though Tom had behaved well the entire day?

To gain pearls of wisdom, try to answer the question on your own before referring to the answer given below.

Answer

1. Harry meant that when he had told Tom that his behaviour was against how God wanted His children to behave, Tom had found his behaviour justifiable. However, when it was the case of the gold coin, he was ready to go to great lengths to keep his temper.

53

King Solomon's Justice

King Solomon, the son of David, was a very wise man. Once, two women came to him with a baby. Each claimed that she was the baby's mother. They wanted King Solomon to give them justice. It was almost impossible to determine who the baby's real mother was.

But King Solomon was a very wise king. He asked for his sword. He told his servants to use it to cut the baby into two equal halves and give one to each woman so that both would have one part.

Hearing this, both the women spoke. King Solomon now knew who the real mother was.

---------------------- **Pearls of Wisdom** ----------------------

1. What did the women say?

2. How did King Solomon know who the baby's true mother was?

To gain pearls of wisdom, try to answer the questions on your own before referring to the answers given below.

Answers

1. One women told King Solomon to go ahead and cut the baby into two, while the other women pleaded that the baby should be spared and given to the other woman.

2. It was easy to make out who the real mother was. The mother of the baby would never be able to bear its death, whether or not it was with her. Thus, the woman who pleaded that the baby be spared and be given to the other woman was the baby's true mother.

STORIES
on
SIKHISM

54

Guru Nanak and His First Deal

When the boy Nanak became old enough to stand on his feet, his father called him and said, "Now you must start earning a living for yourself. Here, take this money and go to the market. Look for a good bargain and see that you earn a profit."

Nanak and his friend went into the market. On the way, they came across a few hungry fakirs. Nanak saw how hungry they looked and his heart went out to them. He and his friend went out to the nearby market and bought them food.

When they reached home, his father asked him, "How was your first day in the market, Son? What was the deal you struck?"

Nanak then told his father that he had bought food with the money he had given him and distributed it to the poor. This only made his father very angry.

"Why have you have wasted my hard-earned money?" asked his father.

———————— **Pearls of Wisdom** ————————

1. What did Nanak say then?

To gain pearls of wisdom, try to answer the question on your own before referring to the answer given below.

Answer

1. Nanak answered, "What can be more profitable than giving to the poor?"

55

Lalo and Malik Bhago

Guru Nanak and his friend Mardana travelled from village to village spreading the lessons of love and tolerance.

They reached a village called Saidpur. There, they stayed at the hut of a carpenter called Lalo. The rich people in the village were shocked at how Guru Nanak could choose a lowly carpenter's hut to stay instead of staying at their houses and benefitting from their hospitality.

One of the rich men was a greedy man called Malik Bhago. He wanted Guru Nanak to come and stay in his mansion. He sent his servant to invite the Guru. But Guru Nanak refused his invitation. This angered Malik Bhago and he asked his people to bring Guru Nanak to him.

When Malik met Guru Nanak, he asked him, "Why did you not accept my invitation?"

Guru Nanak calmly said, "Give me some sweets from your house." When Malik gave him the sweets, Guru Nanak took some bread which he had brought from Lalo's house. He squeezed both of them. Everyone was astonished to see that on squeezing the bread, drops of milk fell from it and on squeezing the sweets, drops of blood fell from them.

Guru Nanak explained...

Malik Bhago was ashamed of his behaviour.

Pearls of Wisdom
---

1. What was the explanation Guru Nanak gave?

2. What can we learn from this story?

To gain pearls of wisdom, try to answer the questions on your own before referring to the answers given below.

Answers

1. Guru Nanak said, "Lalo's simple bread has been earned honestly through his hard work. But the sweets from your house have been made out of the blood, toil and sweat of the poor.

2. For Guru Nanak, the comforts that the rich could give him held no meaning. Instead, he preferred the hospitality of the one who was honest and hardworking and who could offer him only the little that he had honestly earned.

56

Dunichand and the Needle

Dunichand was a rich merchant who lived in Lahore. Once he heard that Guru Nanak had arrived in Lahore and went to meet him. He invited Guru Nanak to his house for lunch. Guru Nanak accepted the invitation.

When Guru Nanak arrived, Dunichand was extremely happy. He made Guru Nanak comfortable and served him lunch. Now Dunichand was in reality a very proud and pompous man. When Guru Nanak began to eat, he said, "I have very expensive cutlery in my house." Guru Nanak said nothing.

Next Dunichand said, "The animals I own are of the best breeds." Still Guru Nanak said nothing. "The statues in my house are priceless," said Dunichand once again.

After lunch, Guru Nanak gave him a needle. "What is this for?" asked Dunichand. "When you die, come to meet me in heaven with this needle," said Guru Nanak.

"But Holy Sir, how can I keep this needle with me after my death?" asked Dunichand surprised.

──────── **Pearls of Wisdom** ────────

1. What did Guru Nanak say to him?

2. What can we learn from this story?

To gain pearls of wisdom, try to answer the questions on your own before referring to the answers given below.

Answers

1. Guru Nanak said, "If you know that you cannot carry anything with you after your death, what is the need to accumulate so much of wealth? Why be proud about it? Use your wealth to help the poor and the needy."

2. We are so engrossed in the accumulation of wealth that we hardly stop to think whether we really need so much. Instead, we can keep aside what we require and spend the rest to help the poor and the needy.

57

How Guru Nanak Chose His Successor

Bhai Laihna was a true devotee of Guru Nanak. When Guru Nanak was to appoint a successor, he knew for sure that Bhai Laihna was the right person. But his wife insisted that he give his sons a chance.

Once, Guru Nanak was passing through a forest with his sons and disciples. Soon they came across a pond. The pond contained water which was contaminated and dirty. Guru Nanak dropped one of his vessels in the pond. He asked his sons to get the vessel out of the water. But the sons refused saying that the water was very dirty and they had so many vessels that it wouldn't matter if didn't bring back that particular vessel.

Then Guru Nanak asked Bhai Laihna to bring the vessel. Bhai Laihna immediately jumped into the dirty pond and brought out the vessel.

_____ **Pearls of Wisdom** _____

1. Who did Guru Nanak choose as his successor and why?

To gain pearls of wisdom, try to answer the question on your own before referring to the answer given below.

Answer

1. Guru Nanak chose Bhai Laihna as his successor. This was not because Bhai Laihna had obeyed him while his sons had not. It was because Guru Nanak compared the dirty pond water as the water containing people's sins. The world needed a Guru who would jump into the dirty water of people's sins and save them without thinking about himself.

58

Guru Nanak's Last Message

Guru Nanak was revered by both Hindus and Muslims alike. When Guru Nanak left this world, both, Hindus and Muslims fought over how his last rites should be performed.

Finally, when both of them went to where his body lay, covered by a sheet, they found that where his body had been, there now lay a bed of flowers.

---------- **Pearls of Wisdom** ----------

1. What was the message that Guru Nanak had given them through this incident?

To gain pearls of wisdom, try to answer the question on your own before referring to the answer given below.

Answer

1. Guru Nanak had always said that God does not belong to any one particular religion. The name of God was supreme and all his life, he had spread God's message of love towards all human beings. That is why people of either religion could not claim his remains as theirs.

59

Guru Nanak and the Fields

Once Guru Nanak and Mardana went to Hardwar. There they found people standing in water facing the sun. Guru Nanak asked them what they were doing. "We want peace for our ancestors. We are throwing water towards the sun to ensure that they find peace."

Guru Nanak then got into the water, bent down and started throwing water in the opposite direction. "What are you doing?" asked the people surprised.

"I am watering my fields in Punjab," said Guru Nanak.

One of the people asked him, "How is it possible for this water to reach Punjab?"

Guru Nanak asked him, "If the water you throw can reach the sun which is millions of miles away and bring peace to your ancestors, then my fields are only in Punjab which is not very far away."

---------------- **Pearls of Wisdom** ----------------

1. What was the message that Guru Nanak was trying to give through this incident?

To gain pearls of wisdom, try to answer the question on your own before referring to the answer given below.

Answer

1. Guru Nanak was trying to make people understand that doing hollow rituals is of no use. Instead of following these rituals after their elders' death, people should be caring, loving and respectful towards their elders when they are alive. Once they are gone there is nothing we can do for them.

60

Guru Arjan

Emperor Jahangir's son Prince Khusro had rebelled against his father. Prince Khusro asked Guru Arjan for help. Guru Arjan agreed to help him. Using this incident some people who were against Guru Arjan took advantage of this and poisoned Emperor Jahangir against Guru Arjan.

Emperor Jahangir asked Guru Arjan to be brought to the court. Guru Arjan was charged with helping the rebellious Prince Khusro. The Maulvis and Pandits also accused him of insulting their religion and their worship.

Guru Arjan replied that he had indeed helped Prince Khusro because Prince Khusro had asked him for help and was in dire need. The Emperor then asked Guru Arjan to remove the offending verses from the holy Granth Sahib.

Guru Arjan firmly replied that there was no such verse in the holy Granth Sahib which could hurt the sentiments of Hindus and Muslims and therefore no change could be made in it.

This angered Emperor Jahangir who had him put behind bars. After a few days, once again Guru Arjan was offered his freedom if only he would remove the offending portions from the Granth Sahib.

The Guru replied that the Granth Sahib had been compiled to lead people to happiness and therefore contained nothing offending and that nothing could be changed in it.

As a result, the Guru had to undergo punishments as well as physical torture. But he bore what came his way with absolute calm. When Miah Mir, a saint and a friend of the Guru visited him in prison, he was aghast to see what the Guru had been put through. He was unable to see the Guru's sufferings and burst into tears.

Miah Mir asked him, "I know you have powers which you can use against your enemies and escape from prison. Why then do you suffer this torture at their hands?"

Pearls of Wisdom

1. What was the Guru's reply?

To gain pearls of wisdom, try to answer the question on your own before referring to the answer given below.

Answer

1. The Guru said, "It is indeed possible for me to escape. But unlike me, there are others too who are suffering to uphold the truth. My suffering shall inspire those who are ready to suffer for their beliefs."

61

Mardana and Guru Nanak

Mardana was a devoted follower of Guru Nanak. He had been with the Guru for 47 years and had accompanied him wherever he had gone to spread the word of God.

Once while they were on their way from Sultanpur to Lahore, Mardana asked Guru Nanak if he could go into a village and ask for something to eat. The Guru permitted him to go.

The kind villagers not only gave Mardana plenty of food, they also gave him a bundle of clothes. Mardana brought the food and clothes to Guru Nanak.

Guru Nanak saw the food and clothes and told Mardana…

─────────── **Pearls of Wisdom** ───────────

1. What did Guru Nanak say to Mardana?

2. What was the reason behind doing so?

To gain pearls of wisdom, try to answer the questions on your own before referring to the answers given below.

Answers

1. Guru Nanak told Mardana to distribute the excess food and the clothes to the poor and the needy.

2. The Guru did not want Mardana to accumulate unnecessary things received in charity. Doing so would encourage a person to be greedy and such a person was of no use to others.

62

God Himself Helps Us

A king once asked Guru Nanak, "Guru*ji*, you had once said that God Himself helps His devotees. But why must He do that? Doesn't He have so many disciples and prophets? Why doesn't He ask them to help His devotees?"

Before Guru Nanak could answer, the King's young son slipped and fell into the river. Immediately, the King got up and jumped into the river and brought out his child.

Once the child was safe, the King came back to the Guru and resumed his conversation. Then Guru Nanak asked him, "O King, we were having a conversation just now. Why did you suddenly jump into the river?"

The King said, "My son had fallen into the river. I went to save him."

Then Guru Nanak said, "But you have so many servants don't you. Couldn't you send any one of them to save your son?"

The King said, "My son is most precious to me. I can't take any risks in this matter and so I went to save him myself."

Then Guru Nanak explained...

Pearls of Wisdom

1. What did Guru Nanak say?

To gain pearls of wisdom, try to answer the question on your own before referring to the answer given below.

Answer

1. Guru Nanak said, "O King! It is the same way with God. His love for his devotees is just like your love for your son and that is why He Himself helps His devotees!

63

The Panj Pyare

Guru Gobind Singh, the Tenth Guru, had decided to fight the Mughals and drive them out. He gave the Sikhs the cry of 'Sat Sri Akal' – God is Truth. He decided to create an army of saint soldiers.

In the year 1699, on the first day of Baisakhi, he told his Sikhs to assemble. A large crowd of Sikhs came. Guru Gobind Singh addressed the crowd and said, "For this army, I am in need of one head. Who will volunteer?"

There was pin drop silence. Then a youth stood up and said, "I will volunteer, Guru. Take my head." The Guru took him into a tent. After a while, the Guru came out of the tent alone and his sword was dripping with blood.

"I want another head," said the Guru. After pin drop silence again, another man volunteered. "Take my head, Guru." The Guru went into the tent with the man and after some time reappeared alone with his sword dripping with blood. The crowd was astounded.

"What is the Guru doing?" they thought.

Then in the same way, the Guru asked for three more heads. Three more people volunteered and the crowd was stunned. After taking the fifth man with him into the tent, the Guru came out of the tent with his blood-stained sword.

"What has happened to those five men? They are nowhere to be seen and the Guru's sword is dripping with blood. What does the Guru want?" the crowd thought.

Then the Guru went into the tent once more and brought out the five volunteers. He explained...

--------------------- **Pearls of Wisdom** ---------------------

1. What did the Guru say?

2. What did the incident mean?

To gain pearls of wisdom, try to answer the questions on your own before referring to the answers given below.

Answers

1. The Guru said, "These five fearless volunteers are my *Panj Pyare* – my beloved five. Their courage and faith forms the basis of a new community – *The Khalsa* or the Pure."

2. The Guru wanted to appoint the five disciples or *Panj Pyare* and was testing the crowd. He was looking for courage, fearlessness, sacrifice and faith and he found it among the five volunteers. The names of the *Panja Pyare* were: Bhai Daya Singh, Bhai Dharam Singh, Bhai Himmat Singh, Bhai Mukham Singh and Bhai Sahib Singh. The Guru gave *Amrit* to the *Panj Pyare* and baptised them.

64

Guru Tegh Bahadur and the Imposters

Guru Hari Rai, the Seventh Guru, had chosen his youngest son, Har Krishan to succeed him as the Eighth Guru. When Guru Har Krishan was in Delhi, an epidemic of small pox broke out. Guru Har Krishan personally went to help the suffering people but he succumbed to the disease. Before his death, he said the words, 'Baba Bakale' indicating that his successor would be Tegh Bahadur who would be found in the town of Bakala.

On hearing the news of Guru Har Krishan's death, Tegh Bahadur and his wife and mother paid their last respects to him and returned to Bakala where Tegh Bahadur went into meditation. But 22 other imposters grabbed this opportunity and called themselves the next Guru and set up their courts to attract followers.

Meanwhile, a trader called Makhan Shah was returning home from the turbulent seas. There was a great storm and his ship was in grave danger. Frantically, he prayed that he would donate 500 gold coins to the Guru if he safely landed at the port. He was saved and when he came in search of the Guru at Bakala to fulfil his promise, he found not one but 22 Gurus. He understood that they were imposters and that he had to find the right Guru.

He went to each of the impostors and offered them a single gold coin each. Each of them took the gold coin and asked him to become their disciple. Then Makhan Shah came to know about Tegh Bahadur and went to meet him.

When he met Tegh Bahadur, he immediately came to know that he was the True Guru.

_____ **Pearls of Wisdom** _____

1. How was Makhan Singh convinced that Guru Tegh Bahadur was the True Guru?

To gain pearls of wisdom, try to answer the question on your own before referring to the answer given below.

Answer

1. While the rest of the imposters happily pocketed the single gold coin that Makhan Shah offered them, Guru Tegh Bahadur reminded Makhan Shah of his promise of offering 500 gold coins. He told him to fulfil his promise like a true devotee. The imposters were not even aware that Makhan Shah had made such a promise. Only the real guru, Guru Tegh Bahadur, had known about it. Hence, Makhan Shah knew that Guru Tegh Bahadur was the Real Guru.

65

Humayun and Guru Angad Dev Ji

After the death of Babar, his son Humayun became the Mughal Emperor. But after some time, Sher Shah who had an eye on the throne declared war against Humayun. Humayun was defeated in this war but he escaped.

When Humayun reached Lahore, he wanted to meet saints. He believed that if they prayed for him, he would get back his throne. He was told that Guru Nanak had prayed for his father's success and his prayer had been granted by God. He too wanted to meet Guru Nanak. But he came to know that Guru Nanak had left for his heavenly abode and Guru Angad was his successor.

So, Humayun decided to meet Guru Angad. He took plenty of presents for Guru Angad. But when he reached the Guru's place, he did not get down from his horse. Even in the Guru's presence, he remained seated on his horse. He was expecting that the Guru would come to meet such a famous ruler like him.

At that time, Guru Angad was meditating and didn't notice Humayun. This angered Humayun. "A simple fakir dares to insult a ruler like me!" he thought. "It's an insult. He deserves to be punished." Thinking so, he brought put his sword to cut off the Guru's head.

Just then, Guru Angad opened his eyes. He looked at Humayun and said...

Humayun was ashamed and begged his forgiveness.

———————— **Pearls of Wisdom** ————————

1. What did Guru Angad say to Humayun?

To gain pearls of wisdom, try to answer the question on your own before referring to the answer given below.

Answer

1. Guru Angad said, "Oh Humayun, it is surprising that your sword, which can so easily kill defenceless fakirs, was powerless against Sher Shah."

66

Nanak and His Thread Ceremony

When Nanak grew into a young boy, his parents arranged for his thread ceremony. However, when the priest came towards Nanak with the sacred thread in his hands, Nanak refused to wear the thread.

Nanak's parents, his relatives and people who had come for the thread ceremony were shocked at how he could refuse to wear the thread.

In answer to their question, Nanak began to sing...

> *If you have a sacred thread whose cotton is Mercy,*
> *Thread is Self-control,*
> *Knot is Determination, and*
> *Twist is Truth, please give it to me.*

People were surprised at his words. Nanak explained to them.

Everybody was stunned into silence and they did not force him to wear the sacred thread.

Pearls of Wisdom

1. Why did Nanak ask for a sacred thread with these qualities?

To gain pearls of wisdom, try to answer the question on your own before referring to the answer given below.

Answer

1. Nanak wanted to emphasize that mere rituals meant nothing. He asked the priest for such a thread because, a sacred thread whose cotton was mercy, thread was self-control, knot was determination, and twist was truth, could never break, would never get dirty, would never burn and neither could it be lost. While the usual thread would only be worn by the body, these qualities would also benefit the soul of the wearer.

67

Guru Nanak and the Bowl of Milk

Once during their travels, Guru Nanak and Mardana reached the city of Multan. Multan was known for the many holy men who lived there. Many people came to them to seek solutions to their problems and gave them gifts and money. When the holy men came to know that Guru Nanak had arrived in Multan, they were worried. They did not want their popularity to reduce. So, they decided to send him a message.

They sent him a messenger with a bowl filled up to the brim with milk. With the bowl was the message, 'There are plenty of holy men here. There is neither room nor need for any more.'

The messenger asked Guru Nanak if he had any message to give to the holy men. Guru Nanak picked a jasmine flower and dropped it in the bowl. The flower floated on the milk without even a drop of it spilling. The Guru Nanak gave the messenger his message for the holy men.

Pearls of Wisdom

1. What was the message that Guru Nanak gave the holy men?

To gain pearls of wisdom, try to answer the question on your own before referring to the answer given below.

Answer

1. Guru Nanak's message was, "Just like there is enough place in this bowl for this flower, similarly, there is always place in the world for good things. There is enough place in this world for everyone."

68

The Successor of Guru Amar Das

A man called Jetha came to meet Guru Amar Das when he was at Goindwal. The Guru's teachings inspired Jetha and he stayed with the Guru. Later, he also married the Guru's daughter.

When it was time for the Guru to choose a successor, he decided to choose between his two sons-in-law. He told them that both of them would have to build a platform as per his directions.

Both of them accordingly built platforms. But when the Guru inspected them, he said, "Destroy both of them and build new platforms again."

So both of them again built platforms. But once more, the Guru said, "Destroy both of them and build new platforms again."

Even though the platforms were built the third and fourth times, the Guru said the same thing. Now the elder of the Guru's son-in-laws gave up. But Jetha went on building platforms for the fifth, sixth and seventh times until at last the Guru was satisfied. No doubt, the Guru declared that Jetha would be his successor. He gave Jetha the name Ram Das (servant of God). Guru Ram Das became the Fourth Guru of the Sikhs.

————— **Pearls of Wisdom** —————

1. Why did the Guru chose Jetha as his successor?

To gain pearls of wisdom, try to answer the question on your own before referring to the answer given below.

Answer

1. The Guru chose Jetha because of his consistent hard work and patience. He was a true devotee and did not mind the hardship that befell him. He continued to do his best till his Guru was satisfied with his work.

69

Guru Nanak and the Non-Vegetarian Food

Guru Nanak was against the spread of the hypocrisies and rituals that were carried on in the name of religion. Once, he was travelling through a holy place of the Hindus called Kurukshetra. It was the day of the solar eclipse and a large number of devotees had entered a lake for a purifying bath.

Guru Nanak asked Mardana to cook deer meat. Once the meat was cooked, he asked Mardana to distribute it among the devotees. The devotees were shocked. That they had been served meat at a holy place like Kurukshetra was unbearable for them.

This irked them and they gathered together with the intention of causing harm to Guru Nanak. However, Guru Nanak was unaffected.

When they asked him for a clarification, he replied...

The crowd bowed down before him and dispersed.

—————————— **Pearls of Wisdom** ——————————

1. What did Guru Nanak say to the people?

2. What is the moral of this story?

Answer

1. Guru Nanak said, "Only fools argue over whether or not to eat meat. They are unaware of the truth. Who defined what constitutes meat and what constitutes plants? Who decided whether eating meat is a sin or not?"

2. Guru Nanak wanted to create awareness in the people that it was very difficult to distinguish between vegetarian and non-vegetarian diets. Like animals, even plants and vegetation were full of life. Therefore, there was no sin in eating food originating either from plants or animals.

70

Nanak and the Fields of Grain

As a boy, Nanak was very kind and helpful. He would do whatever he could to help others. Once his neighbour asked his father if he would send Nanak to watch over his fields as he had to be away for a few days.

His field was full of ripe crop which he had to soon harvest but in the meantime, he had to be away. He was afraid that if someone didn't look after his fields, the birds would eat all the grain and there would be nothing left to harvest.

He asked Nanak's father for Nanak's help and Nanak readily agreed. The farmer went on his way happily. Nanak went to his neighbour's field to watch over it. Nanak went and sat in a *machaan*. The fields were full of ripe grain. In some time, hundreds of birds began to come and peck at the grain and eat it.

Nanak believed that the whole world belonged to God and so he did not feel like shooing away the birds. On the contrary, he was overjoyed to see the birds chirping and eating their fill of the grain. This inspired poetry in him and he began to sing praises of God. Sensing that they were in no danger here, even more birds flocked to eat the grain.

The same thing happened the next day too. Thousands of birds ate up almost all the grain from the fields. When the farmer came back the next day, he was aghast to see that the birds had eaten up all the grain in the field. He was shocked that Nanak hadn't done justice to his trust in him. Now he became very angry and went to Nanak's father to complain.

Nanak's father too was shocked to know that Nanak had not done his job properly. He called Nanak to find out what had happened. The farmer was bursting with rage and shouted at Nanak, "My field would have yielded at least 10 sacks of grain this year. Now due to your carelessness, the birds have eaten up all the grain. I won't even be able to harvest enough food for my family this year. Now what will I eat?"

But Nanak was calm. He said, "Sir, please do not worry. This year you will be able to harvest more crop than you do every year. Please harvest your crop and let me know how much less crop you have harvested."

The farmer thought that Nanak was taking this problem lightly. Tight-lipped, he walked away. A few days later, he harvested whatever was left of the crop in his field. To his amazement, he saw that he had harvested 12 sacks of grain. He wondered how he had been able to harvest so much of grain in spite of the fact that there had been no corn in his field.

He went to Nanak and asked him, "Almost all the crop was eaten by the birds. Then from where have these 12 sacks of grain come?"

Nanak told him. The farmer was ashamed of himself and begged Nanak's forgiveness.

——————— **Pearls of Wisdom** ———————

1. What did Nanak say to the farmer?

To gain pearls of wisdom, try to answer the question on your own before referring to the answer given below.

Answer

1. Nanak said, "These birds belong to God and I had told them to eat the grains which belonged to God and not those from your field. The grains they ate belonged to God. The grain that belonged to you remained untouched in your field."

71

Lehna and the Fruits

Once, Guru Nanak and his disciples had been travelling for two days and had yet found no village and had had nothing to eat. Guru Nanak was unfazed by this, but his disciples were restless with hunger.

Finally, they rested under a canal. There was a tree nearby. Guru Nanak saw that there was something under the tree. He said to his disciples, "Look there. There seems to be something to eat under that tree. Go and see what it is and eat it."

When the disciples went to the tree they saw that whatever was under the tree was covered by a sheet. They were taken aback by this. One of them said, "Oh my goodness! This looks like a dead body. Dead bodies are covered by such sheets."

Then another said, "So are we to eat this dead body now?" A third said, "How will our Guru ask us to eat a dead body? At least take the efforts of removing the sheet to find out what is beneath it."

But no one dared touch the sheet. Lehna who was Guru Nanak's ardent disciple, came ahead and said, "No matter what lies beneath the sheet, I shall definitely eat it." Saying so he took off the sheet.

——————— **Pearls of Wisdom** ———————

1. What had made Lehna remove the sheet and resolve to eat what was below it, when the others were hesitant?

When Lehna removed the sheet, the disciples saw that under the sheet were delicious fruits. Everybody jumped for joy and began eating the fruits. Lehna took two mangoes and went to his Guru and said...

——————— **Pearls of Wisdom** ———————

2. What did Lehna say to Guru Nanak?

3. What is the moral of this story?

To gain pearls of wisdom, try to answer the questions on your own before referring to the answers given below.

Answers

1. Lehna had complete faith in his Guru. He was completely devoted to him and wanted to fulfil his orders with complete faith. He knew that his Guru would only tell him what was right for him and so he had no fear of what he would find under the sheet and whether it would be edible or not while the other disciples were full of doubts and so, were hesitant to lift up the sheet.

2. On finding the fruits, all the disciples rushed to eat them. But Lehna remembered that like all of them even his Guru

hadn't eaten anything since the last two days. He took the two mangoes to Guru Nanak and requested him to have them. The disciples on the other hand, had completely forgotten about their Guru with whose blessings they had found the fruits.

3. If one becomes a disciple, one's submission to one's Guru must be complete. Lehna had no fear of a dead body. He completely trusted his Guru's words. At the time when food was finally before them, Lehna was able to overcome his hunger and think of his Guru first before eating the fruits himself. His unswerving devotion towards his Guru and his selflessness was the reason that Guru Nanak chose him as his successor. Lehna became Guru Angad Dev, the second Guru of the Sikhs.

72

Guru Nanak and the Guard

Guru Nanak travelled far and wide to spread the word of God. He also travelled as far as Mecca, Medina and Baghdad. One day, when he was resting at Mecca, his feet were pointing towards the holy Kaaba.

One of the guards saw this and angrily said, "How dare you point your feet towards the holy Kaaba?"

In a humble tone, Guru Nanak said, "Kind sir, please forgive me. I am extremely tired and did not realize what I was doing. Could you please…?"

The guard understood his mistake and begged Nanak's forgiveness.

───────── **Pearls of Wisdom** ─────────

1. What did Guru Nanak say to the guard?

2. What can we learn from this story?

To gain pearls of wisdom, try to answer the questions on your own before referring to the answers given below.

Answers

1. Guru Nanak said, "I am extremely tired. Could you lift my feet and place them in the direction where there is no God?"

2. God's presence is not restricted to a certain place or a certain direction. God is all-pervading. He is in each and everything and there is nowhere where He is not present.

73

Guru Nanak and the Sesame Seed

Guru Nanak's teachings were inspiring many people to join him and soon he came to be known far and wide. Wherever he went, people from those villages came and gave him various gifts, food, etc. But Guru Nanak did not keep any of these things with him. Whatever he received, he would it distribute it among his disciples or the people in the villages.

Even though Guru Nanak had many disciples, there were also people who thought he was cheating people and misguiding them. Among such people was a renowned *sadhu* who thought that there was no truth in Guru Nanak's teachings.

Once, the *sadhu* decided to test Guru Nanak. When he met Guru Nanak, he place a single sesame seed on Guru Nanak's palm. He wanted to see what Guru Nanak would do with the single sesame seed.

Guru Nanak understood that the *sadhu* was testing him. He called Mardana and said, "Sadhu Maharaj has given me this sesame seed. Please cut it and put it in a vessel filled with water and distribute the water among everybody."

Pearls of Wisdom
---

1. What did Guru Nanak prove to the sadhu by doing so?

To gain pearls of wisdom, try to answer the question on your own before referring to the answer given below.

Answer

1. Guru Nanak believed in distributing and sharing everything he received from others. The *sadhu* wanted to see what he would do with a single sesame seed. But by asking Mardana to put the seed in water and distribute the water among everybody, Guru Nanak was able to distribute the single sesame seed among everyone else.

STORIES
on
BUDDHISM

74

Increase Your Periphery

A man who was disappointed with life once came to Buddha. He told him that he was totally disappointed with the way his life had turned out and asked the Buddha if there was a solution.

Buddha asked the man to take a handful of salt and put it in a glass of water and drink the water. When the man did so the Buddha asked him how it tasted. The man made a face and said it was salty and awful.

"Now take another handful of salt and mix in the water of the lake and then drink it," said the Buddha. After the man did so, the Buddha asked him, "Now how does it taste?

"Sweet," said the man.

"Didn't you taste the salt you had mixed?" asked the Buddha.

"No, I couldn't taste any salt," said the man.

The Buddha asked, "Did you learn anything from this incident?"

——————— **Pearls of Wisdom** ———————

1. What was the message that Buddha was trying to give through this incident?

To gain pearls of wisdom, try to answer the question on your own before referring to the answers given below.

Answer

1. The pain, sorrows and disappointments we face in life are like the salt. But when our periphery is limited to a glass of water, the pain, sorrows and disappointments seem overwhelming and unbearable. But when we increase our periphery to that of a lake, the same amount of pain, sorrows and disappointments are hardly noticeable. So, to get over your pain, increase your periphery.

75

Let My Son Live!

An old woman once came to see Buddha. "My young son, aged 25, just died yesterday. He was my only support. I can't live without him. Please bring him back to life."

The Buddha looked at her calmly and said, "Fine. I will do so. But for me to do that, it is important that you find me a family where there has never been any death till now. Bring me such a family and I will restore you son to life."

The woman went away happy. She set off on her search to find such a family. After a few years, she came back to the Buddha. "Did you find such a family?" he asked.

Pearls of Wisdom
---

1. What was the woman's reply?

2. What is the moral of the story?

To gain pearls of wisdom, try to answer these questions on your own before referring to the answers given below.

Answers

1. The woman replied that she had travelled far and wide but had not been able to find a single family where there had been no deaths. Every family had lost someone or the other.

2. Each one of us has to go through the eternal cycle of birth and death. What is here is not there tomorrow. No matter how unfair it may seem or whether we understand it or not, we must learn to take death, whether our own or that of our loved ones into our stride and learn to accept the inevitable.

76

Gautam Buddha and the Brahmin

Once when Buddha was meditating under a tree, a Brahmin came to him and began to hurl abuses at him.

However, Buddha remained calm. This infuriated the Brahmin and he once more began to abuse Buddha. But even the expression on Buddha's face did not change.

Now the Brahmin was truly furious. He shouted at the Buddha, "I have been abusing you for so long but aren't you angry at me?"

In an equally calm voice Buddha replied, "I have not accepted any abuses from you."

"But didn't you hear them?" asked the Brahmin.

Buddha said, "Your abuses still remain with you, my friend. They did not reach me at all. So why should I get angry?"

"How is it possible?" asked the Brahmin.

Buddha then asked the Brahmin…

───────────── *Pearls of Wisdom* ─────────────

1. What did Buddha ask the Brahmin?

2. What is the moral of the story?

To gain pearls of wisdom, try to answer the questions on your own before referring to the answers given below.

Answers

1. Buddha asked the Brahmin, "If someone gives you a gift and you don't accept it, who does the gift belong to?"

2. No one can insult you until you accept his insults. The Brahmin hurled abuses at Buddha but since Buddha did not accept his abuses, there was no reason for him to get angry at the Brahmin.

77

Buddha and the Young Men and Women

Once, Buddha was staying in a garden. Some young men and women happened to come there for an outing. One of the young men was not married and was accompanied by a prostitute who was young and very beautiful.

While everybody was busy enjoying themselves, the prostitute gathered everyone's valuables and ran away. When everybody realized that the girl had stolen their belongings and run away, they began to search for her.

On their way they saw Buddha and asked him, "Did you see a young girl running? She has stolen our valuables. We are looking for her."

Buddha smiled in his usual way and said...

---------- *Pearls of Wisdom* ----------

1. What did Buddha say?

2. What is the moral of the story?

To gain pearls of wisdom, try to answer the questions on your own before referring to the answers given below.

Answers

1. Buddha said, "Friends, instead of looking for the errant woman, do you not feel it important to look into yourselves first?"

2. It is very easy to call someone a culprit and try to punish the person for it. But if we look into ourselves, we may realize that the culprit was able to harm us because we were not conscious and aware. Introspection is the key to increase our awareness.

78

Prince Sattva and the Tigress

This is the amazing story of Prince Sattva. It is said that he was one of the previous incarnations of Gautam Buddha. Through he was a prince, he renounced his kingdom to become an ascetic.

Once while he was walking with his disciple, they came to a cliff's edge. They looked down and saw a tigress with her newborn cubs. The tigress was starving and was contemplating eating her newborn out of sheer hunger.

Sattva told his disciple to go and look for food for the tigress. The obedient disciple went to look for food but Sattva realized that it would be difficult for him to find food for a tigress.

To ensure the survival of the tigress and her cubs, Sattva jumped off the cliff. The hungry tigress ate him up. When his disciple came back to the spot, he couldn't see his guru anywhere and realized that his master had given up his life for the sake of the hungry tigress and her cubs.

Then, he understood why his master had sent him away. He bowed to his guru for being the epitome of sacrifice and compassion.

────────── **Pearls of Wisdom** ──────────

1. What were Sattva's thoughts while deciding on the
   sacrifice?

_To gain pearls of wisdom, try to answer the question on your own
before referring to the answer given below._

Answer

1. Sattva was moved to compassion for the tigress and her cubs.
   He wanted to prevent the tigress from eating her cubs. He
   realized that to appease the tigress' hunger, someone else would
   have to give up his life. He thought that after all, his body was
   only flesh and blood and by giving up his life, he could save
   the tigress from eating her cubs and also do his duty.

79

Prince Siddharth and the Swan

Once upon a time, Prince Siddharth (as Gautam Buddha was called before his renouncement) and his cousin Devdutt were playing in the palace gardens. Suddenly, they saw some beautiful swans flying.

Devdutt took out his bow and shot his arrow at the swans. As Prince Siddharth watched, one of the swans fell down at his feet. He picked up the swan and saw that an arrow had struck its wing.

With great care, he took out the arrow out of the swan's wing. He lovingly washed the swan's wound and bandaged it with his shirt.

While he was busy saving the swan's life, Devdutt came running looking for the swan. Seeing the swan in Siddharth's hands, he said, "That's the swan I shot. Give it to me."

"I won't give it to you," said Siddharth.

"But it's mine. As per the law of the kingdom, I shot it so it's mine," said Devdutt.

"Yes it is the law, but this swan is not dead. It is only injured and I will try and save it," said Siddharth.

When they couldn't come to any conclusion, they decided to go to the king and ask him for justice.

"It's my swan because I shot it," said Devdutt.

"That law applies only if the bird were dead. But it is only injured and I saved it," said Siddharth.

Now the question was – who did the swan belong to? The ministers discussed the problem but couldn't reach a conclusion. Just then, an old man came in the court and said, "I can help you decide." He took a look at the swan and said...

—————— **Pearls of Wisdom** ——————

1. What did the old man say?

To gain pearls of wisdom, try to answer the question on your own before referring to the answer given below.

Answer

1. The man said, "This swan would want to be free and be with other swans. It would want to live. And so the swan should be given to the person who saved it."

80

Women in the Sangha

Ananda was a trusted disciple of Lord Buddha. He played an important role in shaping the Sanghas and spreading the message of Buddha.

Earlier, many women expressed the wish to join the Sangha. But they weren't allowed to do so because their presence could distract the monks from their paths. But, Ananda did not think this was right. He thought this was discriminating against one gender.

Buddha clarified that he too was against discrimination. However, the effect of some inborn instincts was very difficult to ignore and overcome. He felt that the Sanghas should be restricted only for monks. But Ananda answered his doubts and convinced Buddha to allow women into Sanghas.

―――――――――― **Pearls of Wisdom** ――――――――――

    1. What did Ananda say to convince Buddha?

―――――――――――――――――――――――――――――

To gain pearls of wisdom, try to answer the question on your own before referring to the answer given below.

Answer

1. Ananda said, "Our path leads to Nirvana. But by not allowing female monks, we are denying the path of Nirvana to half the human population. If we preach that all human beings are equal, how can we ourselves treat men and women differently?"

81

Buddha's Visit to Kapilvastu

Many years after Siddhartha attained enlightenment and became Buddha, he came to the capital of his kingdom, Kapilvastu. The King and Queen were informed that Prince Siddhartha had come back. This made them very happy and they went out to welcome their son.

They expected that after achieving his spiritual quests, Siddhartha would take up his kingly duties and other family responsibilities as well. They made arrangements to give him a grand welcome. But contrary to their expectations their son came along with a group of monks asking for alms.

"O King, please give me alms," said Buddha. The shocked King said, "What alms, my son! All that I have, this kingdom, this palace, is all for you and you alone. Why then do you ask for alms?"

Buddha said, "O King! I have renounced my kingdom, my relatives and all things that bind me. I am not here as your son. I am a monk. I eat what I can get as alms to stay alive. Of what use are these riches to me?"

"But son, what about your duty towards your parents, your family, your child?" asked his mother. "Aren't you ignoring these duties of yours?"

——————— **Pearls of Wisdom** ———————

1. What did Buddha reply?

Then he went to his wife and said, "Respected Lady, I seek alms." He offered his bowl to her. Buddha's wife Yashodhara was seeing him after ages. She thought for a while and...

——————— **Pearls of Wisdom** ———————

2. What did Yashodhara place in Buddha's bowl as alms and why?

To gain pearls of wisdom, try to answer the questions on your own before referring to the answers given below.

Answers

1. Buddha said to the Queen, "I am not ignoring my duties, O Queen. Rather, I am increasing the scope of these duties. Let us all rise above personal and emotional bonds and try to improve the lives of all mankind. Let all children be our children. Let us love all parents like our own."

2. Yashodhara brought their son Rahul and placed his hands in Buddha's bowl. She understood Buddha's quest for Nirvana and wanted her son to follow his father's path. Hence, she offered him to Buddha, asking him to accept his son in the Sangha.

82

Buddha and the Elephant

Buddha's cousin Devdutt was jealous of him. He decided to kill Buddha. He knew when Buddha was supposed to pass through a specific town. Before Buddha's arrival, Devdutta brought an elephant into the town. He gave it liquor so that it would be drunk.

When he saw Buddha approaching, Devdutt hit the drunk elephant with all his might. The hurt elephant was totally enraged. Devdutt then freed the elephant so that it rushed towards Buddha, trumpeting loudly.

On seeing the mad elephant charging at them, Buddha's disciples ran away from the spot to save their lives. But Ananda remained with Buddha. Buddha saw the enraged elephant and stood where he was. He was calm and peaceful.

Just a few steps before reaching Buddha, the elephant suddenly stopped and became calm. Then it went towards Buddha and bowed respectfully to him.

——————— **Pearls of Wisdom** ———————

1. How had Buddha been able to stop the mad elephant?

To gain pearls of wisdom, try to answer the question on your own before referring to the answer given below.

Answer

1. Buddha felt compassion and kindness for the elephant. His being radiated his love and warm feelings to the distraught animal and it calmed down immediately.

83

Buddha and Amrapali

Once, during his travels, Buddha reached the city of Vaishali. It was an alluring city and was home to the beautiful dancer Amrapali. She was very popular and had numerous admirers. Though she was rich, she was fed up with the material world and so she sought spiritual wisdom. She had heard of Buddha and his teachings and had been influenced by them.

When she heard that Buddha had come to Vaishali, she was very happy and eager to meet him. She went to the garden where Buddha was meditating and stood before him. She stared at his calm and peaceful face.

When Buddha opened his eyes, he saw her face innocent and devoid of any desires. He asked her, "Lady, what can I do for you?"

Amrapali folded her hands and said, "Lord, I am Amrapali, a court dancer. I have come to invite you for a meal at my house tomorrow. I hope you will not mind eating at the home of a court dancer."

Buddha said, "O Lady! Your social standing makes no difference to me. Your invitation is sincere and genuine and I shall be pleased to accept it."

Amrapali was very happy and was rushing home to make

preparations for Buddha's arrival. On her way, she came across some princes. They were astonished to see her rushing and asked her where she was going in such a hurry. She happily told him that she was going to make arrangements as Buddha was going to come to her house for a meal.

This shocked them. They were on their way to invite Buddha for a meal. They were surprised how Buddha had accepted Amrapali's invitation.

The princes met Buddha and extended their invitation to him. But he said, "Sorry, young men, I have already accepted Amrapali's invitation."

One of the princes said, "Do you know that she is a court dancer? A dancer's house is no place for a holy man like you." When Buddha replied, the young princes were ashamed.

Pearls of Wisdom

1. What did Buddha say to the princes?

To gain pearls of wisdom, try to answer the question on your own before referring to the answer given below.

Answer

1. Buddha said, "The royal court is also no place for a monk like me. Then why have you come to invite me for a meal?"

84

The Right Path to Happiness

While on his travels, Buddha met an ascetic who was doing penance while standing all the while. Buddha asked him, "Holy Sir, will you please tell me why you are troubling your body so much."

The ascetic said, "I am doing these austerities so that the sins of my past births may be destroyed; no new sins shall be committed by me in this birth and finally, I will be rid of all my sorrows."

Buddha asked him, "Do you know who you were in your last birth?"

The ascetic said, "No."

"Do you know what sins you had committed in your last births?"

"No," replied the ascetic.

Buddha said, "Can you tell me how many of your sins and sorrows have been destroyed and how many remain?"

The ascetic said, "No. I can't tell you that."

Then Buddha said…

———————   *Pearls of Wisdom*   ———————

1. What did Buddha say?

2. What is the moral of this story?

To gain pearls of wisdom, try to answer the questions on your own before referring to the answers given below.

Answers

1. Buddha said, "If you do not know the answer to these questions, aren't all your penances and austerities a waste?"

2. To ensure that we do not commit sins in the future, introspection is necessary. Introspection would help us to see our mistakes and make us aware so that we do not commit them in the future. This introspection can only be done in solitude. Buddha preached that introspection and solitude and not penance and austerities are the true means to enlightenment.

85

Enlightenment for Everyone

In Buddha's times, the religious and social situations were truly challenging. The Kshatriyas and Brahmins were occupied in rituals and atrocities. The common people were caught up in the bondage of traditions, customs and casteism.

Buddha had achieved enlightenment. He preached this knowledge to the common people in a very simple way, explaining that the root cause of all sorrow was desire. However, some religious scholars were of the opinion that Buddha should not share this knowledge with the common people. They felt that this would only cause the common people to leave their earlier rituals, customs and traditions and adopt new customs. In short, apart from changing the rituals that bound them, nothing else would be achieved.

Lohitya, a Brahmin from Shalvatika village was also of this opinion. Once, he invited Gautam Buddha for a meal. During the meal, Buddha asked him, "Do you think that if one acquires some specific knowledge, one should experience it oneself and not share it with others?" Lohitya replied that it was indeed so.

Then Gautam Buddha asked him, "Friend, the king has gifted you this village. Would it be correct to say that the produce of this village, its resources, and all the money it earns belong to you alone? Are you the sole owner of everything that the village produces? What about those who depend on the farm produce and the trade in the village for their livelihood? Would it be fair to them?"

Lohitya said, "Not at all, O Holy One! It is important for every villager to obtain his share in the produce of the village. Denying him his share would be doing a grave injustice to him."

——————————   **Pearls of Wisdom**   ——————————

1. What did Gautam Buddha reply?

To gain pearls of wisdom, try to answer the question on your own before referring to the answer given below.

Answer

1. Gautam Buddha said, "Similarly Lohitya, denying others the knowledge of the path of enlightenment is doing a grave injustice to them. Everybody has a right to this knowledge."

86

Buddha and the Ignorant Students

Buddha was completely against people who would make use of ambiguous statements and fictitious philosophies to cheat the common people. He would challenge religious scholars to explain their statements.

Once, three Brahmin students came to him. They had a difference of opinion about which was the right way to worship 'Brahman'. All of them were firm that the method explained by their respective gurus was the right one. All of them were trying to prove the superiority of their respective gurus. In the end, they could not establish who amongst their gurus was superior. All of them decided that they would ask Gautam Buddha for the right answer and establish the superiority of their gurus.

Gautam Buddha said, "Friends, have you ever seen Brahman yourselves?"

They all replied in the negative.

"Then what about your gurus who have taught you the different ways of worshipping Brahman? Have you ever heard of them seeing Brahman?"

"Never, O Holy One!" they replied.

Then Buddha said, "Suppose a young man were to tell you that he was in love with the most beautiful woman on earth. Out of curiosity, you ask him who she is, how she is, where she lives and he replies that he is unaware of all these things, but still he is in love with her. Would it be right on his part to make such a statement?"

"Not at all," agreed the youths.

"If you are unaware of where to construct a building, would it make sense to argue about how its staircase should be designed?"

"Absolutely not," said the youths.

Then Buddha said...

———————— **Pearls of Wisdom** ————————

    1. What did Buddha say?

    2. What was Buddha trying to tell the students?

To gain pearls of wisdom, try to answer the questions on your own before referring to the answers given below.

Answers

1. Buddha said, "Then friends, would it be wise to extensively debate on the method of worshipping that about which we have absolutely no information?"

2. Buddha was telling the students that they were wasting their time arguing on fictitious philosophies and trying to establish the superiority of their gurus. Instead, they should stop their arguments and accept the path of introspection which would lead to enlightenment.

87

A Farmer by Intellect

Buddha used to sustain himself by asking for alms. At such times, many people would tease him or even display their anger and hatred towards him. But their attitude would make no difference to him. Buddha would answer such mischief mongers in his usual calm and serene way. However, on hearing his answers, people would take back their words and beg his forgiveness.

Once, Buddha went to the house of a farmer and asked for alms. The farmer was rich as well as arrogant. He said to Buddha, "My dear man, we work hard in the fields. For what do we put in our blood and sweat? To hand over the crop to people like you? Why don't you too work hard in the fields?"

Buddha calmly said, "My friend, like you, I too am a farmer."

In a fit of anger the farmer said, "What a fine farmer you are! You have no farm, no animals and no plough!"

Buddha said, "My dear fellow, how can you say that I do not have these things?" And he explained how he too was a farmer.

———————— **Pearls of Wisdom** ————————

1. What did Buddha say?

To gain pearls of wisdom, try to answer the question on your own before referring to the answer given below.

Answer

1. Buddha said, "The conscious of the sorrowful, miserable people is my farm. I plough the fields of their minds, remove the thorns and weeds of ignorance and sow the seeds of belief in them. Then this farm gives me the divine crop of Nirvana. So, like you, I too am a farmer."

88

Buddha Achieves Nirvana

There was a village called Pava where an ironsmith called Chandu used to live. One day, he invited Buddha to have a meal at his home. But unfortunately, the food in his house had gone bad. So as soon as Buddha consumed it, he fell very ill.

His disciples laid him on a bed below a *Shal* tree. Buddha understood that his end was near. In a very low voice, Buddha told Ananda, "For me, the alms I received when I attained enlightenment and the alms I received today are the same. Please tell this to Chandu."

Seeing Buddha in this state pained all his disciples and the villagers. Everyone was drowned in sorrow. But even in his last moments, Buddha was calm as ever.

Pearls of Wisdom
---

1. Why did Buddha ask Ananda to tell Chandu that the alms received when he attained enlightenment and the alms received from Chandu were the same for him?

To gain pearls of wisdom, try to answer the question on your own before referring to the answer given below.

Answer

1. Buddha knew that the food served by Chandu had gone bad.
   He knew that if Chandu came to know that Buddha had died
   due to the bad food, he would regret it for the rest of his life.
   Secondly, people would also blame Chandu for being the cause
   of Buddha's death. So he gave the message to Ananda so that
   Chandu would not blame himself and neither would people
   blame him for Buddha's death.

89

Buddha and King Bimbisara

Before Buddha got enlightenment, he had once met King Bimbisara. On knowing that Prince Siddhartha was seeking enlightenment, King Bimbisara had told him, "O Prince, if you receive enlightenment, please do come to meet me and guide me." Promising the king that he would come to meet him, Siddhartha went on his way.

After Siddhartha achieved enlightenment and became Buddha, a lot of people were inspired by his teachings and became his disciples. Among his disciples was the great Rishi Kashyap who understood Buddha's teachings that merely following rituals would not lead to enlightenment.

Once, when Buddha, Rishi Kashyap and his other disciples were passing through a jungle, they came to know that King Bimbisara was planning to perform a huge *yagna* (fire sacrifice) and that animals were going to be sacrificed for the *yagna*.

At the same time, King Bimbisara was happy to know that Buddha and his disciples were very close to his kingdom. He went to meet Buddha. Buddha said to him, "O King! You had told me to come to guide you about the right path, after I receive enlightenment."

King Bimbisara said, "I am organising a big *yagna*. I have come to invite all of you to attend this *yagna*."

Buddha replied, "O King! Sacrificing blameless animals is not the way to enlightenment."

King Bimbisara was surprised at Buddha's words. But he turned to ask Rishi Kashyap for guidance and said, "O learned Sir, what is your opinion?"

On hearing Rishi Kashyap's words, King Bimbisara said to Buddha, "I shall not go ahead with this sacrifice. Please accept me as your disciple and show me the path to enlightenment."

——————— **Pearls of Wisdom** ———————

1. What did Rishi Kashyap say?

2. What is the significance of this story?

To gain pearls of wisdom, try to answer the questions on your own before referring to the answers given below.

Answers

1. To King Bimbisara's utter surprise, Rishi Kashyap said, "O King! My Guru has already told you that doing fire sacrifices and killing innocent animals is not the path to true enlightenment."

2. King Bimbisara was under the impression that Buddha had received enlightenment after becoming Rishi Kashyap's disciple. So when Buddha told him not to sacrifice animals for the *yagna*, King Bimbisara asked Rishi Kashyap for his opinion. But he was shocked to know that the learned Rishi Kashyap had himself become Buddha's disciple.

STORIES

on

JAINISM

90

Lord Parshvanath

The king of Varanasi, Ashwasen, had a son named Parshva Kumar. Parshva Kumar later became the 23rd Tirthankar, Parshvanath.

When Parshva Kumar was a child, there lived a mendicant named Kamath. He was an orphan and had gone through many troubles in his life. Out of his disillusionment, he became a monk and undertook severe penance. Once, he came to Varanasi to perform the *Panchaagni* (five fires) ritual. On hearing this, many people came to worship Kamath.

When Parshva Kumar came to know of this, he realized that living beings were being sacrificed for the *Panchaagni* ritual. He decided that he had to stop Kamath from sacrificing living beings for the sacrificial fire. But Kamath paid no heed to Parshva Kumar. Through his intuition, Parshva Kumar came to know that there was a snake in the sacrificial fire. He decided to save it. But by the time his men brought the snake out, it was half-burnt and died immediately.

Parshva Kumar immediately recited the *Navkara Mantra* and the snake was reborn as Dharanendra, the king of the Asur Kumars. Kamath felt insulted by this but he could do nothing. For the rest of his life, he continued his severe penances. After his death, he was reborn as Meghmali, the Lord of Rain.

On the other hand, Parshva Kumar renounced his kingdom, his family and his worldly possessions and became a monk at the age of 30. He spent his days in meditation and came to be known as Lord Parshvanath.

Once while he was deep in meditation, Meghmali, the Lord of Rain, saw him. He suddenly recollected that Parshvanath was Parshva Kumar and that in his last birth as Kamath, Parshva Kumar had created obstacles in his penance. He saw his chance for taking revenge. He showered all types of harmful and wild animals on Lord Parshvanath.

But this did not affect Lord Parshvanath at all. Disappointed, Meghmali showered heavy rains in an effort to drown him. But then too, Lord Parshvanath remained unaffected. Soon, the water came up to Lord Parshvanath's neck.

Around this time, the snake who was present as Dharanendra noticed this. He quickly brought a fast-growing lotus and placed it below Lord Parshvanath's feet so that He would not drown. Additionally, by spreading his fangs, he created an umbrella to shelter the Lord from the heavy downpour.

No matter how hard he tried, Meghmali was unsuccessful in his revenge. Finally, he realized that it was he who was creating trouble for Lord Parshvanath while Lord Parshvanath was completely detached from his revenge. He sincerely repented his acts and begged Lord Parshvanath for forgiveness.

——————— **Pearls of Wisdom** ———————

1. What qualities did Lord Parshvanath demonstrate?

To gain pearls of wisdom, try to answer the question on your own before referring to the answer given below.

Answer

1. Firstly, by dissuading Kamath from sacrificing living beings in the sacrificial fire, Lord Parshvanath spread the message of non-violence. Secondly, when Meghmali was trying to exact his revenge, he demonstrated complete detachment. He gave the message that no matter how people behaved towards us, we should be detached and unbiased towards them. Both these qualities are essential for Self-Realization.

91

Lord Arishtanemi (Neminath)

Lord Arishtanemi was born in the Yadav dynasty along with Shri Krishna. He was Shri Krishna's cousin. He was the son of King Samudravijay. Since childhood, his nature was quite detached.

The king of Mathura, Bhojavrishni, had a son called Ugrasen. Ugrasen's daughter was called Rajamati. When Rajamati came of age, her parents began to look for a groom for her. Though they thought that the handsome and modest Arishtanemi was the perfect groom for her, they knew of his feelings of detachment from the world right through his childhood and so they were not keen on the match.

On the other hand, when Arishtanemi's parents brought up the topic of his marriage, he too did not take it seriously. His father also knew of his detachment. So he asked Shri Krishna to look into the problem. Shri Krishna assured the King that he would look into the matter.

Shri Krishna spoke to his wife Satyabhama about it. She arranged for a function in spring. Shri Krishna, Arishtanemi, the other Yadavas, Satyabhama and others had all gathered for the function. Satyabhaama, her friends and the others targeted Arishtanemi and taunted him with their comments.

When the ladies went too far with their comments, Arishtanemi laughed at them. Satyabhaama purposefully inferred that Arishtanemi was ready for marriage. Shri Krishna gave the good news to Arishtanemi's father who then asked him to find a good match.

At this time, Rajamati's name was proposed as a good match for Arishtanemi. Everyone was happy with this match. On the decided day, the groom's marriage party reached Mathura.

King Ugrasen had collected thousands of animals and birds which were to be a part of the feasts for the groom's party. This was considered a sign of affluence and status. These animals were mournfully screaming and bleating in fear. On the one hand, the marriage procession created a delightful atmosphere whereas on the other, the screaming animals created a terrible sound. The people who passed through that path turned a deaf ear to the cries of the animals.

But the one person who couldn't do that was Arishtanemi. When his chariot reached the place where the animals were kept, he was moved by their horrible plight. He asked his charioteer why the animals had been locked up and were bleating in fear.

His charioteer explained that the animals were soon to be slaughtered for the marriage feast. Arishtanemi was horrified to hear this. He was extremely troubled and wondered why so many animals were being killed for no apparent reason.

He refused to be the cause behind this bloodshed. He told his charioteer to open the fences, free the animals and then take him back to Dwarka. When Arishtanemi was questioned about his actions, he said...

Pearls of Wisdom

1. What did Arishtanemi say?

To gain pearls of wisdom, try to answer the question on your own before referring to the answer given below.

Answer

1. Arishtanemi said, "Only freedom brings true happiness. Just like these animals were prisoners in the fence, we are also prisoners of our karmas. I wish to move out of this bondage and achieve eternal bliss."

92

Bharat and Bahubali

Lord Rushabhdev (the First Jain Tirthankar) had two wives. One of his wives had 99 sons and a daughter. Bharat was the name of his eldest son and his daughter was called Brahmi. Bahubali and Sundari were the children of his second wife. Both, Bharat and Bahubali were strong and mighty.

As time went by, Lord Rushabhdev felt that he should handover his responsibilities and his kingdom to his children and take up the spiritual path. He gave Ayodhya to Bharat, Takshshila to Bahubali and various small parts of his kingdom to the rest of his sons. Brahmi and Sundari renounced the world and followed their father on the spiritual path.

Bharat was ambitious and wanted to extend the boundaries of his kingdom. He prepared his huge army and developed an extraordinary wheel – the *Chakraratna*. Then he set out on his conquests. He easily gained control over various kingdoms on his route. But for his conquest to be complete, he also needed his brothers to surrender to him. All his brothers surrendered before him and went on the path of spirituality.

But Bahubali did not. His pride would not let him surrender. He also knew that his army would be an equal match for Bharat's army. In spite of the counsel of their advisors, both the armies stood face to face, ready for battle. Seeing the large-scale destruction that the war would cause, the advisors of Bharat and Bahubali finally advised them that since this war was between two brothers and not their armies, they should choose a duel instead of involving their armies and creating bloodshed.

Both, Bharat and Bahubali agreed to a duel without involving their armies. Bharat tried all that he knew to defeat Bahubali and establish his superiority, but he was defeated. Desperately, he tried to hurl the *Chakraratna* at Bahubali, but the wheel did not even touch Bahubali.

Now Bahubali was angered. He picked up his brother and was about to dash him to the ground when he realized what he was doing. He remembered that his father had given up all his riches and prosperity to go on the path of eternal bliss. So had his brothers and sisters. And here, he was thinking of killing his brother whom he truly loved and respected!

He changed his mind then and there and decided to give up all his belongings, his kingdom and worldly possessions and follow his father, brothers and sisters on the spiritual path. But he also realized that if he went to his father, he would have to bow down to his brothers because they had renounced their belongings earlier and so they were senior to him.

He decided that he would seek enlightenment on his own and began to meditate on the spot. He meditated with all his concentration. After some time, creepers began to grow on his feet. One year passed this way, but even then Bahubali did not achieve enlightenment.

On seeing this, Lord Rushabhdev sent Brahmi and Sundari to guide him. Both of them came to Bahubali and told him, "Brother, get off the elephant."

Pearls of Wisdom

1. Where was the elephant?

2. What can we learn from this story?

To gain pearls of wisdom, try to answer the questions on your own before referring to the answers given below.

Answers

1. Bahubali was perched on the elephant called 'Ego'. It was his ego which had not allowed him to go to his father and brothers when he had decided to renounce the world. Even now, his ego was the barrier between him and enlightenment.

2. Just like the shackles of ego had bound Bahubali and would not let him proceed on the path to enlightenment, our ego too binds us to various possessions, feelings, emotions, and the past. Once we overcome this ego, we become humble and can progress on the path to enlightenment.

93

Anand and Gautamswami

A householder called Anand lived in a city called Vanijya. He was extremely rich and had wealth equivalent to that of the king. He was liked and respected by everyone.

One day, Anand attended a sermon given by Lord Mahavira. He then decided that he would accept the twelve vows of a householder. After fourteen years of following the vows, he decided to retire from all his responsibilities. He handed over all his responsibilities to his children and decided to spend the rest of his life in meditation. Due to the purity of his austerities, he attained *Avadhijnan* (Limited Divine Knowledge).

At this time, Gautamswami (Lord Mahavira's disciple) was asking for alms. He heard that Anand was not in good health and had attained Divine Knowledge and went to meet him.

Anand saluted Gautamswami from where he lay on his bed and told him what he had attained. He told him that he was able to see upto the 12th *Devloka*. Gautamswami was surprised to hear this and said that it was impossible for a householder to attain this knowledge. He told Anand that he was lying and that he should repent for it.

Anand on the other hand had not lied at all. In a very humble

manner he told Gautamswami, "I am speaking the truth, Guruji."
But Gautamswami was not convinced. He went to Lord Mahavira
and reported their discussion.

Lord Mahavira said, "Anand is right. Indeed he has achieved
Avadhijnan. It is you who are mistaken. You must ask for his
forgiveness." Gautamswami went to Anand and apologised for
his mistake.

—————————— **Pearls of Wisdom** ——————————

1. What can we learn from this story?

*To gain pearls of wisdom, try to answer the question on your own
before referring to the answer given below.*

Answer

1. The story shows us three aspects of behaviour that we can
   adopt:

   a. Even though Anand knew that Gautamswami was
      mistaken, he brought this to Gautamswami's notice in a
      very humble manner.

   b. Once Gautamswami learnt of his mistake, he went to
      Anand and asked for forgiveness. In spite of the fact that he
      was an accomplished monk, he had no ego.

   c. Lord Mahavira did not defend or condone the mistake of
      his disciple Gautamswami. Rather, he upheld the truth and
      asked him to go and beg Ananda's forgiveness.

94

The Statue of Bahubali

Shravanabelagola hosts a huge statue of Bahubali which was built by his brother, King Bharat. Next to the statue of Bahubali stands the statue of a lady named Gullikayajji. Legend has it that a military leader called Chamundarai decided to bathe Bahubali's statue with milk. For this purpose, the proud Chamundarai arranged for milk in huge quantities.

But surprisingly, when the milk was poured over the head of the statue, it only went till Bahubali's waist. Chamundarai's people tried their best to ensure that the milk would reach Bahubali's feet. They poured huge quantities of it. But to no avail.

Then a simple woman called Gullikayajji asked for permission to pour a small portion of milk over the god's statue. The little offering that she made to the lord not just drenched the entire statue of Bahubali, it also flooded the entire basin.

Pearls of Wisdom

1. How was the small amount of milk poured by the lady able to drench the huge statue?

To gain pearls of wisdom, try to answer the question on your own before referring to the answer given below.

Answer

1. The small amount of milk was poured by the woman with true devotion. There was no ego or arrogance in her behaviour. Although Chamundarai wanted to offer milk to the god, he had not been able to overcome his ego.

95

The Birth of Lord Sumatinath

This is the story that occurred during the birth of Lord Sumatinath, the Fifth Tirthankar. King Megh of Ayodhya was very happy that his queen was expecting.

One day, two women came to the king with a very young boy. Their husband, a rich merchant, had died leaving them with the child. Each woman claimed the child to be hers. One of the women even claimed that the other wanted custody of her son so that he would inherit all his father's wealth.

The child himself was too young to understand who his mother was as both of them had loved him equally. There was no eyewitness available either to help the King decide.

The King was worried. Try as he might, he couldn't solve the problem. He was afraid that in case of a wrong decision, the real mother and the child would be punished forever. His queen observed that he was worried and asked him for the reason. The King narrated the reason and the court's inability to come to a conclusion.

The Queen said, "My Lord, allow me to solve this problem." The King agreed and the next day, the Queen came to court. She understood why the King had been confused. There was no outward indication of any one woman being the real mother of the child.

Suddenly, inspiration struck and the Queen said, "Since this is a very confusing case, I declare that the matter should be kept pending. My womb carries a pious soul. Let this wait till this soul takes birth and is in a position to make a decision on this matter. Till then, the child and the property of the merchant will be kept in custody of the Prime Minister. Both the women will have to wait till then."

One woman immediately accepted this decision. But the other was inconsolable. With tears in her eyes she said, "I can't live without my son. Please don't separate us. Let the other woman be his mother and claim all the property, but please don't separate us."

The Queen immediately gave her decision. The King realized that the enhancement of the Queen's wisdom was due to the presence of the pious soul in her womb and named the new born son Sumati (wisdom).

──────── **Pearls of Wisdom** ────────

1. What was the Queen's decision?

2. What is the moral of the story?

To gain pearls of wisdom, try to answer the questions on your own before referring to the answers given below.

Answers

1. The Queen said that the woman who could not bear to be parted from her son was the real mother. The other woman was more attached to the wealth and so she had immediately agreed to the Queen's decision of keeping the decision pending.

2. The Queen knew that the real mother would not be able to bear her son's absence till the time the decision was made. She would certainly be ready to give up her rights as a mother and plead to the Queen to not separate her and her child.

STORIES
of
SAINTS

96

Shri Shankar Maharaj and the Doctor's God

Yogiraj Shri Shankar Maharaj was a Siddhayogi. He belonged to the *Nathpanth* and is revered as one of the greatest saints in Maharashtra. He was known to be a maverick. He had a devotee called Dr. Dhaneshwar. The doctor had an idol of Lord Balkrishna which he lovingly worshipped.

Lord Balkrishna would talk to Dr. Dhaneshwar. He would eat the *prasad* the doctor placed before Him. This made the doctor truly happy. He would think, *It is my deep devotion which has even made this idol turn live. Just like Lord Vitthal ate Sant Namdev's* prasad, *my Balkrishna too has eaten my* prasad. *Now, I too am a great devotee like Sant Namdev.*

But after some time, he began to wonder. *Is all this true or is it just a figment of my imagination?* He asked Lord Balkrishna, "If this is really true, give me a sign. Give me proof that it is indeed true."

After some days, he saw the sign. Lord Balkrishna Himself ate the *prasad* offered to Him. Additionally, He also removed the gold bangle from His hand. The doctor picked up the gold bangle in his hands. This was a solid gold bangle. But his mind told him, *This is not the truth.*

The doctor was perturbed. He sat down to meditate and began to introspect. Then he did something very unfathomable. He picked up the idol of Lord Balkrishna and threw it out of the window.

From behind him, Shri Shankar Maharaj clapped his hands with glee and said, "Doctor's God is finally dead!"

The doctor also laughed with him.

Pearls of Wisdom

1. Why did the doctor throw his beloved idol out of the window?

2. Why did the doctor laugh with Shri Shankar Maharaj?

To gain pearls of wisdom, try to answer the questions on your own before referring to the answers given below.

Answers:

1. The doctor realized that what was happening was not the truth, but a result of his indomitable will power. It was indeed *Maya* and soon, he would be engulfed by this *Maya*. Soon, his attachment to this *Maya* would become arrogance and he would deviate from the path of introspection and self-realization. To avoid this, he picked up the idol and threw it out of the window.

2. The doctor himself realized that his pride that he was as great a devotee as Sant Namdev, was taking the place of devotion and soon, arrogance too would follow. He did not want to go on the path of pride and arrogance. So, he had thrown

the idol out of the window. Now he was relieved that along with the idol, he had also thrown away his arrogance. He was happy that now he was safe and free to pursue the path of Self-Realization and so, he laughed with Shri Shankar Maharaj.

97

When 'I' Die

Once, a man who was a devotee of Shri Shankar Maharaj came to him asking him for help. "What is it that you want me to do for you?" asked Shri Shankar Maharaj.

The hapless man said, "I am trying very hard to fix my daughter's marriage, holy sir. I am doing everything that I can. But in spite of all my efforts, I have not yet been successful. Please help me. Please tell me when my daughter's marriage will be fixed."

"Do you think I am an astrologer?" asked Shri Shankar Maharaj sternly.

"No, Maharaj," said the man.

Shri Shankar Maharaj then asked one of his disciples to bring the *gatha* of Sant Tukaram. He flipped through the *gatha* and stopped at a page on which was written an *abhanga* (a devotional song) composed by Sant Tukaram. This was one of the habits of Shri Shankar Maharaj. Instead of giving direct replies to the questions of devotes, he would point out relevant passages in various books as per the devotee's nature and ask them to read out what was written. Accordingly, he asked his disciple to read out the relevant *abhanga* to the devotee. But the devotee was not satisfied.

"O Holy One, if you bless me, I am sure her marriage will be fixed soon. It will happen on the date you tell me Maharaj…"

"Fine. If you must know, your daughter will be married when I will die," said Shri Shankar Maharaj.

"What are you saying, O Holy Sir?" quailed the man. "I want my daughter to be married, but for that how can I hope that you will die?"

Then one of Shri Shankar Maharaj's disciples explained what he meant.

--------- **Pearls of Wisdom** ---------

1. What did Shri Shankar Maharaj mean?

2. What is the moral of this story?

To gain pearls of wisdom, try to answer the questions on your own before referring to the answers given below.

Answers

1. What Shri Shankar Maharaj meant was that the man's daughter would be married when 'I', i.e., the 'I' within him or his ego would die. The man was continuously saying, "'I' am worried about my daughter's marriage; 'I' am doing everything to make it happen." It was his ego which had to die before his daughter's marriage could be finalised. Shri Shankar Maharaj meant that marriages were made in heaven. We are nobody to make them happen.

2. We feel that it is we ourselves who make things happen. This makes us arrogant when we achieve something worthwhile. But instead of saying 'I have done this', 'I will do this' and taking the credit for the actions, we must leave everything to God. Know that you are only the *nimitta matra* or the medium through which God brings about the result.

98

All Creatures Belong to God

Sant Eknath was a saint and religious poet who lived in Maharashtra. Once, he and his followers were going from Varanasi to Rameshwaram. They were carrying the water of the holy river Ganga, to offer it to Lord Shiva.

Their path took them through a thick forest. After a while, Sant Eknath found that he had been separated from his disciples. He thought of waiting for them and sat down to rest as it was very hot. Then he saw a donkey that was dying of thirst. He felt great compassion for the poor creature. He tried to look all around him to see if he could find any water, but there was no water to be seen anywhere.

He could see that the donkey was craving water. He made up his mind, took the pitcher filled with water from the Ganga and poured some water down the donkey's throat. But the donkey was so thirsty that it drank up all the water and then there was none left in the pitcher.

By then, his followers had caught up with him and were shocked to see him giving the holy water to the donkey. They demanded, "This was holy water from the Ganga and we were going to offer it to Lord Shiva. Why did you give it to this donkey? Now what will we offer Lord Shiva?"

Sant Eknath replied...

———————— **Pearls of Wisdom** ————————

1. What did Sant Eknath reply?

2. What is the moral of this story?

To gain pearls of wisdom, try to answer the questions on your own before referring to the answers given below.

Answers

1. Sant Eknath said, "This offering of water which has saved the donkey's life is greater than any other offering that we can give to God."

2. Serving God's creatures in their time of need without any expectations is the best offering we can make to God.

99

Sri Ramkrishna Paramhansa and the Scorpion

Once, when Sri Ramkrishna Paramhansa and his disciples were walking along a river, they saw a scorpion floating on water, struggling to survive.

On seeing this, Sri Ramkrishna felt compassion for the little creature. He lifted the scorpion with his bare hand. The scorpion who was scared, stung him.

The sudden pain made Sri Ramkrishna to drop the scorpion. Once again, it fell into the river where it began to struggle anew. Again, Sri Ramakrishna lifted it with his bare hands and quickly took it to the river bank and moved it to safety. But meanwhile, the scorpion had stung him once more.

His disciples asked him, "Master, when you tried to help the scorpion the first time, it stung you and caused you a lot of pain. Why then did you help it the second time?"

———————— **Pearls of Wisdom** ————————

1. What was Sri Ramkrishna's answer?

2. What can learn from this story?

To gain pearls of wisdom, try to answer the questions on your own before referring to the answers given below.

Answers

1. Sri Ramkrishna said, "It is the nature of the scorpion to sting. Additionally, it was scared for its life. It is my nature to help it. How can I give up nature just because it has stung me?"

2. Sri Ramkrishna's answer shows the compassion that great men have for all living beings. It is in their nature to help all living beings irrespective of the benefit or harm it causes them.

100

Sri Ramkrishna and the Idol of Krishna

Sri Ramkrishna was living in Dakshineshwar in Calcutta. Dakshineshwar was blessed with a number of temples devoted to various gods like Lord Krishna, Lord Shiva and Goddess Kali. The priests of Dakshineshwar would worship these gods daily and ensure that the prescribed rituals were conducted.

One day, the priest who was worshipping Lord Krishna noticed that the leg of Lord Krishna's idol was broken. The priest felt that the idol should be immersed in the holy river Ganga and a new idol should be installed in its place. The other priests also agreed that that was the right thing to do.

They decided to ask Sri Ramkrishna for his opinion. Sri Ramkrishna said…

---------- **Pearls of Wisdom** ----------

1. What did Sri Ramkrishna say?

2. What is the moral of this story?

To gain pearls of wisdom, try to answer the questions on your own before referring to the answers given below.

Answers

1. Sri Ramkrishna said, "We should treat the idol as we would have treated a loved one. Just like we would cure the illness of a loved one, we should repair the idol and use it again for worship like earlier." Sri Ramkrishna himself repaired the broken leg of the idol so finely that nobody could make out that it had been broken.

2. An idol of God represents God Himself. Only when we worship the idol with love, faith and devotion we can benefit from worshipping it.

JAICO PUBLISHING HOUSE
Elevate Your Life. Transform Your World.

ESTABLISHED IN 1946, Jaico Publishing House is home to world-transforming authors such as Sri Sri Paramahansa Yogananda, Osho, the Dalai Lama, Sri Sri Ravi Shankar, Sadhguru, Robin Sharma, Deepak Chopra, Jack Canfield, Eknath Easwaran, Devdutt Pattanaik, Khushwant Singh, John Maxwell, Brian Tracy, and Stephen Hawking.

Our late founder Mr. Jaman Shah first established Jaico as a book distribution company. Sensing that independence was around the corner, he aptly named his company Jaico ('Jai' means victory in Hindi). In order to service the significant demand for affordable books in a developing nation, Mr. Shah initiated Jaico's own publications. Jaico was India's first publisher of paperback books in the English language.

While self-help, religion and philosophy, mind/body/spirit, and business titles form the cornerstone of our non-fiction list, we publish an exciting range of travel, current affairs, biography, and popular science books as well. Our renewed focus on popular fiction is evident in our new titles by a host of fresh young talent from India and abroad. Jaico's recently established translations division translates selected English content into nine regional languages.

Jaico distributes its own titles. With its headquarters in Mumbai, Jaico has branches in Ahmedabad, Bangalore, Chennai, Delhi, Hyderabad, and Kolkata.

SINCE 1946